Published by Chartwell Books Inc.
A Division of Book Sales Inc.
110 Enterprise Avenue
Secaucus, New Jersey 07094

Printed and bound in Hong Kong
By Book Print International
Created and produced by
Sackett & Squire Ltd
2 Great Marlborough Street
London W.1.

Library of Congress 79-52751
ISBN 0 89009 286 9

Best Loved

DOGS
OF THE WORLD

CHARTWELL BOOKS INC.

Best Loved

DOGS

OF THE WORLD

Jennie Chandler

Contents

Introduction

To many people a house is not a home without a dog snuggling beside a roaring winter's fire. At times scampering at your heels during a long summer's walk, or loyally waiting at a gate for your return — these are the traits we have come to expect of these dear friends.

Their faithfulness is acclaimed throughout the world, from the hardy and enduring huskies of the arctic circle to the defensive Lhaso Apso of the Tibetan monasteries.

Few animals vary so much in size, shape, color and temperament as the dog — and much of this diversity results from the selective breeding of these animals over many hundreds of years. They have been bred for every conceivable job, from pastoral duties with sheep and cattle to defending stagecoaches and even to catching fish.

The dog also takes a major place in sport. Setters, retrievers and pointers have all been developed to help man find, flush out and retrieve game birds. While the speedy dogs, such as the Afghan Hound, have been used to overtake and kill fast-running animals like antelope and gazelle.

The slower hounds, including the Bassetts and Beagles, are used against smaller and trail-leaving creatures, which can be trapped finally in a lair or earth. The fearless terriers, while not being especially good at scenting prey, are bold and aggressive when put down a hole or burrow in pursuit of other animals. But such is man's temperament that he has also developed dogs to be nothing more than playthings, for sitting on laps and being admired. However, many of these lap-dogs at one time played an important role in the pursuit of game. For instance, the delightful Cavalier King Charles Spaniel was very active on the Scottish grouse moors, while the Poodle, with its trimmed legs and body, was used to retrieve game from water.

Working dogs are still kept throughout the world, and are used for such activities as pastoral, police and military work, assisting visually handicapped people and protecting property.

This beautiful all-color book features dogs throughout the world, discussing their ancestry and how they have been used by man.

Young Cocker Spaniels are delightful and charming, displaying all the attractive qualities expected of a pup. This well-known gun dog is one of the most famous sporting breeds, as well as being, perhaps, the oldest. During the reign of Queen Elizabeth the First they were used to drive birds and small game into nets. They are gentle and ideally suited to homes with children.

Looking After Your D

g

Choosing a puppy can be one of the most magical moments in the life of a family. What puppy shall be chosen? Should he be large or small, spotted, bearded, or long tailed? These are but a few of the many questions which are bound to arise. Then there is the moment the young animal arrives in your home, and all the family are so eager to make him feel welcome. It is a big moment in your life, and perhaps an even bigger one in the pup's.

The young pup will only be a few months old, and it may be the first time he has left his mother. Therefore, he will need all the love and understanding you can give.

This chapter will guide you through many of the difficulties which are bound to arise, from the time you decide to have a pup and until training him to react to words of command.

The range of breeds available is extensive, and in addition there is always the possibility of buying a mongrel. Many people believe a mongrel is equally as intelligent as pedigree breeds, and this is often quite right. If you are just looking for a pup that will grow up into a family dog, then there is every good reason to buy a mongrel, especially if you know that the mother is a friendly animal, with a pleasant disposition to children.

Few people show their dogs seriously at national dog shows, even though they may have a pedigree breed. There are, obviously, no rigid rules about the best breed to buy to suit your house or personal temperament. Indeed, it is often said that a dog slowly assumes the disposition and appearance of his owner! But whatever the breed, all puppies and dogs need love and an owner who will look after them responsibly.

Poodle puppies are naturally inquisitive and, as with all young animals, eager to explore the outside world, but at the same time rather reluctant to leave their mother. Puppies born in the summer will benefit from a few hours in the sunlight every day, but do take care that shade and water is provided for them.

Left: Cavalier King Charles Spaniels are friendly and soon make friends with other animals. The two stately Abyssinian cats here are welcome, in spite of the superior attitude of the spaniel. Most cats and dogs become great friends if they are brought up together, and often the cats will groom the dogs.

Far left: these St. Bernard puppies are enjoying the fresh air. They will grow into the majestic animals which are world famous for their endurance and feats of rescue. With their expressions of dignity, benevolence and intelligence they immediately capture attention.

Looking After Your Dog

Selecting a dog is very much a personal matter and can be influenced by memories from previous years of a particular breed which attracted the attention. It is quite easy to compile a list of breeds which suit the size of your house, money available to feed him and time required for training and exercising, but usually there is something more emotional and loving between families and their dogs.

There are, of course, certain breeds which are noted for their gentle and tolerant disposition to children, and some of these are, as one might suspect, in the group of dogs which look after sheep. The setters, retrievers and spaniels are also gentle dogs which admirably adapt to a family home. Also, some of the small dogs, such as the Cavalier King Charles Spaniel, like children. But much of the animal's suitability to young children may depend on the way they were treated during their early and formative weeks, and the dispositions of their parents. If possible, always check on the parents of a puppy you are thinking of introducing into a family home.

Buying a Pup

There are three main ways of buying a pup — from a reputable dog breeder, a pet store, or friend. Each of these ways has its advantages and disadvantages, and it is worth looking at them.

Buying from a dog breeder It is best to buy from a dog breeder specializing in the particular breed you want, rather than from a general kennel. Local veterinary surgeons may be able to suggest suitable kennels. If not, write to your national kennel club (enclosing a stamped-addressed envelope) asking for a list of kennels in your area specializing in the breed you want.

Always check over the kennel before committing yourself to buying an animal. Make certain the kennel is clean, with no stale food on the floor, and that all the animals are happy and contented. Also, have a look at the pup's parents, as this will indicate if it would be suitable for children. Don't choose litters where the mother is snappy and surly.

All good kennel owners are interested to know where their animals are going, and if the proprietor enquires about you as much as you ask about his kennel and pups, then this is a good indication that the kennel is reputable.

Buying from a local pet store The great difficulty in obtaining a dog this way is that it is usually impossible to know or see the pup's parents. It therefore follows that the dog's suitability as a friendly family dog cannot be gauged. It is inevitable that animals sold through pet stores are mongrels, and although many are excellent with children, their eventual size is often unknown.

There are good and bad pet stores, but invariably the good ones smell fresh and look clean and have a proprietor who is interested in all of his animals and the homes they are going to. If you are uncer-

tain about the pet's health, have a vet check him over.

Buying from a friend This is an excellent way of getting a pet, as it is probable that you know the pup's mother quite well and can judge her temperament and suitability as a family pet. Also, puppies brought up in a home atmosphere are able to make the change to another home very easily, whereas a kennel-raised pup often takes longer to settle in. Don't be tempted to select the weak pup in the litter just because no one else wants him. If you have any doubts about his health, call in a vet to check him over.

Buying a Healthy Pup

It is essential that the puppy you buy is healthy, alert and happy. A healthy puppy is one that is, perhaps, slightly overweight, but without a pot belly. His nose should be cold and wet, with a pink and clean tongue, alert eyes and clean and white teeth. If the pup has diarrhoea, a cough, runny eyes and does not move easily on all legs, then don't choose him.

Look out for the pup in the litter that is brighter and more alert than his sisters or brothers — that is the best choice.

Bitch or Dog?

Most people have a preference for either a dog or bitch, and both can be equally attractive and friendly. However, it is natural for a dog to be more aggressive and roamful than a bitch. Dogs tend to be more extrovert and interested in other dogs — all year round — whereas bitches are rather more loving and devoted to their homes, except when they are in season.

Bitches come into season or, as it is often called, on heat, twice a year, and at such times are receptive to sexual overtures from the male of the species. Such is their tendency to roam and be generally more frisky at these times that in the Middle Ages they were said to be in their 'Jolly Season'.

A bitch first comes into season between the ages of six and ten months. Smaller bitches tend to take longer. The bitch becomes restless, with a swelling of the vulva, which lasts for five to seven days. This is followed by a discharge of a reddish fluid for four to seven days. It is as the discharge ceases that the bitch is in season and when mating should take place. The bitch only remains able to conceive for three to five days.

It is at these times, if you have a bitch, that you will have to take special care of her and not let her near any dog. Preparations can be bought to hide her natural scent at such times, and dabbing her paws with a strongly smelling substance, such as oil of lavender, when taking her for walks may help to keep dogs away. Also, carry her several yards from your house before putting her down.

Decreasing a Dog and Bitch's Sexual Drive

Both dogs and bitches can be freed of all sexual problems by castrating dogs and spaying (removal of the ovaries) bitches. A castrated dog is likely to be less aggressive and not so liable to wander away, while spaying removes all worries about unwanted puppies.

A dog can be castrated between the ages of six and eighteen months, and a bitch after she has been in season once. If castration or spaying is carried out too early, and before the animal's sexual instincts have developed, they may become fat and lethargic.

Settling in the Pup

It is a traumatic time in a pup's life when leaving the comfort and security of a mother, and at such times love and understanding are needed. It is at this stage that, if pestered by young children, a pup could become snappy and aggressive. So for the first week or two — until he becomes confident of his new surroundings — he should be treated quietly and gently.

He will need a draftproof and warm box, with a soft blanket into which he can snuggle. Some people recommend giving puppies a hotwater-bottle, well and

Above: this Entlebuch Mountain Dog — often called the Entlebucher Sennenhund — and Tabby Cat obviously hold each other in great esteem and respect. Cats and dogs can become inseparable companions, often eating the same food and drinking from the same bowls.

Right: many puppies, such as these young and attractive German Shepherd Dogs, do not closely resemble their parents. When these pups develop into adults they will be alert and watchful, with a high degree of intelligence, and capable of quick movement.

Left: the inquisitiveness and mischievousness of puppies often leads them into amusing situations, especially where food is concerned. This very young Irish Setter obviously cannot resist climbing on to the plate in order to tackle the food from a more advantageous position.

Far left, above: firmly based drinking and feeding bowls are essential for the puppy. All eating and drinking containers must be thoroughly cleaned every day. On no account should food be left in a bowl from day to day. If the pup has long ears, the feeding bowl can be placed on a firm box, so that the ears flop either side, rather than into it.

Far left, below: all dogs like to bite into a bone — it helps to strengthen their teeth and gums. But beware of bones which might splinter and either pierce the gums or be swallowed.

Worming the Puppy

Puppies are usually wormed for round worms when they are three to four weeks old, and this is usually done by the dog breeder before you take charge of your pup. But do check with the breeder to ensure that it has been done.

This first worming is carried out by separating the bitch from the pups. The vet would have been consulted and a prescribed dose of a dog-worming prescription given to each pup. Subsequently, the string-like worms will emerge with each pup's excreta, usually after the next meal. It is essential that the worms are removed and either burnt or flushed down the toilet if they are not to be ingested by the bitch or the pups. Scrupulous care is needed to ensure that you wash your hands thoroughly after this treatment, and children are best kept away from the pups.

The worming is repeated after two weeks.

securely wrapped in a blanket, to cuddle against, while others say this is dangerous as the bottle may burst. However, as long as the bottle is strong and not perished, and is firmly covered, it must be a comfort to the new arrival.

Take care that the box is not placed under a busy table or where hot liquids or other things might fall into it. And check that all small chewable things are removed from his reach.

He will need a firmly-based water dish, refilled with fresh water at least once a day. Also, a feeding bowl that he can reach and get his head into without knocking it over is a requirement. It is essential during these early days that he realizes where his bed is and that he is to sleep in it. Also, make sure that his water and feeding bowls are always in the same place.

Lastly, give him smiles and words of encouragement during his early days — it will make him a more confident and happy dog.

House Training the Pup

It is not difficult to train a pup to go into the garden to attend to his natural functions — but it does require diligence during the early days. After every meal the pup

should be taken into the garden — and always choose the same spot as there is then the chance that the location will remind him of what he is there for. Wait until he has performed, and reward him with a smile and "Good Boy".

If he does have an accident on the floor in the house, then scowl at him and say, gruffly, "Bad Boy". Immediately take him outside to the same spot and encourage him to perform.

Feeding the Puppy

Puppies need careful feeding, and food which is a continuation of their previous diet. It is, therefore, useful to have a chat with the breeder of the puppy you are buying to ask on what and how often he is fed.

It is probable that by the time the pup is sold to you, often between eight and twelve weeks of age, he will be having five meals a day. This is because at this stage he has a small stomach and is unable to digest large amounts of food at one time. From the age of about five weeks to two months the diet could be: *Breakfast*: Cereal and fine biscuit well soaked and mixed with warm milk. Dog meal and a beaten egg can be added to give extra vitamins so necessary for development.

Mid-morning: Repeat the breakfast meal.
Lunch-time, about 2 pm: Lightly cooked burger, tripe, fish or liver, finely chopped and moistened with gravy. Wheat germ capsules and cod-liver oil can be added.
Mid-afternoon: A warm drink.
Early evening: Repeat his lunch-time meal.

It is essential not to over feed him at any of these meals, and any food left in the dish should be removed and thrown away. Also, as the pup gets older, less gravy and milk will be needed.

Between two and four months of age his meals can be reduced to four a day and from five to nine months only three will be needed.

Feeding the Adult Animal

As soon as the animal nears full size, and this obviously varies from breed to breed, only one meal a day plus a bedtime snack is required. Large dogs, by the way, often take up to eighteen months or even two years to reach maturity, whereas small dogs reach their ultimate size between eight and twelve months. Dogs,

like humans, require a well-balanced diet, and not scraps of food left over from meals. Healthy dogs demand a diet of proteins and carbohydrates.

Dogs like a routine, and it is therefore essential to give the main meals at the same time each day. Usually, an early evening meal is recommended, because if he has been active all day a meal at that time encourages him to be quiet during the evening. Dogs look forward to a quick snack at bedtime, and crushed biscuits are ideal.

Exercising your Dog

All dogs need exercise — sporting and large dogs more so than small ones. Puppies, of course, should not be subjected to vast amounts of exercise until they are well developed and their bones firmly formed.

Fat and lethargic dogs are a disgrace to themselves and especially to their owners, who need to take a responsible attitude in this respect. Like routine feeding, the exercise needs to be at regular times each day, so that the animal

Above: most dogs have a natural instinct to dig holes, whether it is to bury a bone or just to create a mess and an interesting cavity in the soil. Dogs usually become more active and playful when on a sandy beach.

Right: many dogs take naturally to water. This Kleiner Münsterlander, the smaller of the German Setters, is brown-and-white and used as a sporting gun dog, when he will often retrieve game from water. While many dogs do take naturally to streams and pools, never force a young puppy or even an adult to go into the water. Young animals are often put off water for life if forced into it.

Above: large dog shows often have classes for each breed. This dog handling class is for German Shepherd Dogs, and although there is usually a high degree of competitiveness between the handlers, the whole atmosphere is one of friendliness. The dogs often sense the competitiveness of such events and perform at their best.

Left: dogs can be trained to undertake many tasks in the service of man. The training programme for such dogs first involves the simplest of commands, followed by commands to retrieve objects. Here, a German Shepherd Dog holds a dumbell used in one of the obedience tests.

expects his daily walk. However, before venturing out into the street with your young animal, he needs to be obedient and to have street manners.

Training your Puppy

Before training him for street manners, make sure that he is house-trained and has mastered the trick of indicating when he wants to go outside. It would be bewildering to the animal to have to learn two different new ideas at the same time.

You will find that your pet is quite easy to train if you are able to let him associate the things he does well with a responsive smile and "Good Boy", or a scowl and "Bad Boy" when he does something incorrectly. Never hit your dog with your hand, although a rolled-up newspaper can be used to chastize him. But best of all, try to rely on smiles and words of encouragement. And the golden rule is that admonishment should be given directly the deed has been done, not hours after when the animal will not be able to associate the punishment with the crime.

Teaching him his name It is essential, of course, that he should be able to respond to his name, as without such ability he will not be able to come to heel on the word of command.

The easiest way to do this is to associate it with food. Every time you put his food down, call his name and when he arrives tell him how good he is. This way he will soon respond to his name.

Training the animal When starting to train the animal, it is essential to find a small and quiet area in your garden where his

attention cannot be distracted. He will already know his name, so stand him in the middle of this area and walk a few paces backwards. Then call his name. He will probably come to you, when he should be praised. When he arrives, make him sit down to the command of sit.

By the way, do not complicate his life with a vast number of different words of command. Select a few, such as "Come", "Sit" and "Lay", which together with his name should enable you to make him an obedient fellow.

Accustoming him to a leash The first step is to get him used to wearing a collar, and this is usually best achieved while he is playing, when he would not be so conscious of it. For the first few times, take it off after a short period, or as soon as he becomes aware of it, but gradually increase the time he wears it. Do remember to take it off at night.

When he has become used to the collar, atach a light leash to it and allow it to trail after the dog. As soon as he is used to it, lift the end of the leash and walk him gently around the garden.

Road and curb drill When he is used to a leash, he can be taken out into the street, This will be a big time in his life and he may well become confused and excited at meeting other dogs.

Do remember that if he should wish to relieve himself while in the street — and most dogs do — that he must attend to his calls of nature in the gutter. It is an offence to allow a dog to foul the public footpath.

Crossing a road with him should be taken in three basic stages: making him sit at the curb, you looking to ensure that no traffic is coming, and then to command him to walk across the road in a steady manner. It is essential to get the animal into a known routine when crossing the road.

Dogs in Cars

Dogs normally take to cars like fish to water, enjoying the exciment of being involved with the family. However, many puppies are sick during their first car ride, and therefore try to accustom them to short rides to start with. Try to make him sit down in the same place, so that he knows what is expected. It is as well to give him a blanket to sit on, in case he is sick.

If after several journeys he still does not travel happily, consult your vet for advice.

Do remember to stop frequently for him to stretch his legs and get some fresh air, especially in the summer. Dogs quickly suffer from overheating, and this is especially so in badly ventilated cars. Also, in the summer remember to park in a shaded spot and to leave at least one of the windows open.

Boarding Kennels

It is inevitable that at some time during the dog's life he will have to spend some time in a kennel. This can often be as traumatic for the dog as for the owner. If you are in any doubt about a good kennel in your area, ask your vet.

Always check that the kennel is clean and the animals are exercised every day. There should be no un-eaten food on the floor and drinking bowls should be clean.

Remember to discuss your dog's diet if he has a special one, and to leave an

Worming the Adult Animal

The worming treatment will have to be repeated when the animal is five to six months old, and on occasions may have to be given again during the dog's life if he shows symptoms of worm infestations. This is indicated by a pot belly, failure to grow, bad breath, or worms or parts of worms in the animal's faeces or vomit.

If worming is needed, consult your vet for a suitable treatment.

emergency address and telephone number in case you are needed urgently.

Biting

It is inevitable that some dogs and breeds are more likely to bite children and adults than others. Some dogs become snappy towards the end of their lives, while others are irritable and aggressive when ill — especially if unnecessarily disturbed.

If your dog is snappy, and especially so with children and visitors, then warn them not to go near him. Should anyone be bitten, go along to your doctor or emergency centre to have the wound treated.

Veterinary Care for Your Pet

It is inevitable that at some time during

their lives pets become ill and require medical treatment. Often, it is easy to see that the animal is in distress, but quite difficult to diagnose the cause, and this is when expert advice from a veterinary surgeon is required. Rather than guess the cause of the dog's illness, quickly call in a vet. Many of the illnesses and disorders which your pet may encounter are set out in this chapter, but remember the golden rule — when your animal is unwell — the sooner treatment is given, the greater the chance of a full and rapid recovery.

Abrasions which are slight can be cleaned with a solution of warm water and an antiseptic, and should then be covered with a bandage. Replace the bandage daily, cleaning the wound at every change.

Abscesses are inflamed and painful swellings, often accompanied by a rise in temperature. Remember not to squeeze the abscess.

Two main methods are usually used to encourage the abscess to burst. First, covering the infected area with hot compresses. Or, secondly, bathing the abscess in a warm solution of salt water. Clean the area with an antiseptic solution when it bursts.

Allergies are complaints which affect dogs as well as humans. Dogs sometimes react unfavourably to things they sniff at or eat, and these can range from certain foods to detergents and plant pollen. The reaction can also be varied, from vomiting to running eyes and red skin.

The best way of treating the animal is, of course, not to allow contact with the substances which trouble him.

Arthritis often affects old dogs, and the best cure is to keep them warm. For severe cases, consult a vet.

Bad breath is often a sure sign that the animal is not well, and if it lasts for more than two or three days, consult your vet. However, if the dog is young and teething, bad breath is quite normal.

Bad breath often indicates a worm infestation, a stomach infection, tonsillitis, a mouth ulcer, broken teeth, a lip infection, or, in elderly dogs, a kidney failure

Apart from seeking medical advice chlorophyll tablets with a dosage of up to six tablets a day — depending on the animal's age and size — can be given.

Bites are usually the result of fights, and if slight can be cleaned with an antiseptic solution. Bad cuts will need the attention of a vet.

Bladder infections in dogs result in a wide range of symptoms. These include abdominal pain, straining to pass urine, loss of appetite, and traces of blood in the urine. Your vet should be consulted at the earliest possible moment.

Broken teeth do not usually hurt a dog, but may often cause dribbling or bleeding from the gums or even bad breath. Consult your vet.

Bronchitis causes excessive coughing. It can be treated with codeine linctus. Consult a vet if, after two days, the dog is still coughing.

Burns and scalds usually happen in the home. If the dog is in shock, keep him warm. A drink of warm water and glucose will help. Badly burned dogs need veterinary help, as secondary infection may occur.

Canker is a very painful condition, caused by tiny parasites in the ear. Often the condition drives a dog to distraction, and

Above: this little Collie puppy will grow up into one of the most famous of all breeds used to shepherd sheep. The name Collie is derived from an old breed of Scottish sheep called Colley. The adult Collies are very intelligent and loyal, often displaying great courage.

Right: Beagle puppies are naturally inquisitive. According to legend, these attractive dogs are descended from scent hounds used by King Arthur and his knights. Beagles are ideal as family pets, as they are small, companionable and very good with children.

Above: these Wolf Spitz puppies are members of the Spitz group, which is formed of breeds such as the Akita Inu, Chow Chow, Elkhound, Husky, Keeshond, Pomeranian, Samoyed, Schipperke, Vallhund and Pembrokeshire Welsh Corgi. Spitz breeds are usually distinguished by a ruff of hair around their necks and a curly and dense tail.

Left: these attractive Miniature Schnauzers have an appeal all of their own. The standard sized Schnauzers are thought to have originated in Württemberg in Bavaria, and were used as cattle drivers and ratters. The miniature version comes from a selective cross between small Schnauzers and Affenpinschers. They are hardy, sturdy and long lived, and make excellent house and watch dogs.

may cause fits of hysteria. Take the dog along to the vet.

Canine hepatitis is a highly contagious virus which attacks dogs. The essential treatment of this disease is to get veterinary advice quickly. Puppies should be inoculated against the virus when eight weeks old. Remember not to allow puppies near other dogs until they have been inoculated.

Choking occurs when the throat is blocked, preventing breathing. In such cases treatment is needed rapidly. Open the dog's mouth and ensure that the tongue is not blocking the throat. If the blockage is due to something the dog has tried to swallow, try to hook it out with a finger: do not push it further down the throat. Call in a vet if it cannot be moved.

Constipation occurs in dogs from time to

time. The dog may be seen to be straining, to bleed, or to vomit. Three or four tablespoons (60-80ml) of liquid kerosene may help, but if he has not recovered within 24 hours, consult your vet.

Diarrhea may be accompanied by vomiting. Withhold water and food for a day or so. If the diarrhoea continues for five days, consult a veterinary surgeon.

Distemper is highly infectious and can affect dogs at any age. The incubation period is from three to fifteen days. Immunity can be provided by annual vaccinations — consult your vet for full details.

Infected dogs are listless, with a high temperature of about 40 deg C (105 deg F). They display a lack of appetite, with a dry cough, discharge from the eyes and, eventually, vomiting and diarrhoea. Con-

sult a vet as soon as possible.

Eczema is an inflammation of the skin. Often, the dog is irritable and bites and scratches his skin, which becomes red and sore. The hair is rubbed away, leaving a bare area.

Apply a solution of one part in a thousand potassium permanganate crystals to the area. Then wash the entire dog thoroughly and dab calamine lotion on the bare areas.

Electric shocks often happen to dogs, especially puppies, who tend to chew cables. If your dog is stretched out near a frayed cable it is likely he has received an electric shock. The first thing to do is to switch off the electricity supply. If this is impossible, push the dog free of the cable, using a broom.

It is probable that the dog has urinated

and this may be conducting electricity, so don't stand in it.

If the dog has not come to, administer artificial respiration.

Eye troubles require professional advice as soon as possible.

Fits can take several forms. Unfortunately, there is very little that can be done for the dog, other than preventing him from hurting himself or attacking and biting anyone. Contact a vet rapidly.

Fleas are often part of a dog's life. They create irritation and annoyance to the dog, as well as transmitting the eggs of tapeworms. Fleas are small, reddish, flat creatures. Infected dogs should be bathed every other day for two weeks. Also, make sure that his bed is clean, dusting it with pyrethrum or derris powder.

Gastritis is stomach inflammation, resulting from over-eating, or eating contaminated food. Symptoms are violent vomiting, accompanied by marked thirst and diarrhea. Keep the dog warm, withholding food and water for a day, then give light foods for a few days. If the trouble persists, seek the advice of a vet.

Hard pad is closely associated with distemper, the basic symptoms being the same, but with the addition of diarrhea and hardening of the foot pads and nose. Consult a vet quickly.

Jaundice occurs when a growth blocks the bile duct, or when a disease prevents the normal secretion of the bile. The animal passes orange urine and has a yellowish coloring of the skin. Take the animal along to your vet.

Leptospirosis is a bacterial disease,

Above: Afghan Hounds are some of the
great characters of the dog world, with
an aloof and dignified expression. These
puppies will soon loose their young,
gangling appearance and become
attractive adults.

Left: the Boxer is considered to be a
cross between the Great Dane and an
English Bulldog, and was developed to
bait bears and to fight wild boars. He is
an outstanding pet and guard, and has a
distinguished gait that makes him appear
to lope along. Boxers, unfortunately,
have the trait of snoring and dribbling.

Right: Retrievers are one of the classic
gun dogs, with a gentle and caring
disposition that makes them loved as
family dogs. They are excellent with
children, who seem to know that they are
safe with them.

Right: the Chow Chow is a distinctive dog with a distinguished past. They are intensely loyal animals and tend to be one-man dogs. With their expressionless faces they appear to be fierce, and have a will all of their own. Because of their abundant coats they are not suitable for warm climates. It is a breed that gained much popularity in Britain when it was favoured by Queen Victoria, and in 1895 the Chow Chow club was formed.

Far right: the Irish Setter is often known as the Red Setter because of the very attractive color of his coat. These puppies are delightful and amusing, but they will probably grow up into highly strung adults needing careful training. It is a breed that loves to show off to visitors, and is a born clown, full of mischief.

A Time to Go

It is inevitable that towards the end of your treasured pet's life it is necessary to make the difficult decision about ending his existence. There is no firm guide as to when a dog is best put to sleep, but usually it is done when the animal is enfeebled through old age or as a result of an illness. It is not difficult to know when an animal is in distress, but the question always arises as to whether he should be put down now, or whether the pet be well and happy enough to go on for a further few months or a year. At such a time, take the advice of a vet, who from vast experience will be able to tell you if your pet is in pain, or if the illness is incurable. If the answer is that for the pet's own happiness he would be best put to sleep, take his advice.

It is far better to save the animal from unnecessary suffering, and for you to remember him as he was when in his prime, than to keep an aged and sick animal. It is a difficult time and a traumatic decision to put an animal to sleep, and a time for much personal courage.

highly contagious and transmittable to humans. Infection is spread from dog to dog through urine. Dogs and puppies are more frequent sufferers than bitches.

Infected animals are lethargic and thirsty, with sore stomachs. It is followed by a high temperature, vomiting and diarrhea.

The only treatment is to get professional help. Call in a vet, and ensure that the family wash their hands after touching the animal.

Lice are flat little creatures which crawl slowly through and around the base of the dog's hair. Treatment is easy. Bath and shampoo the dog every other day for two weeks using a medicated shampoo.

Mange is a skin disease caused by small, eight-legged spider-like creatures called mites. They cause loss of hair, discomfort and toughening of the skin. The dog and his living area should be thoroughly washed every three or four days, but if the mange is still present after two weeks consult a vet.

Pneumonia is a lung infection caused by either a virus, bacteria or worm. It is associated with a high temperature, coughing and general inertia. It is a serious disease, so consult a vet.

Rabies is a serious virus disease. It is transmitted in the saliva of a rabid dog. It is a virus which causes death to infected animals, and an extremely painful series of injections for humans infected by it.

The first symptoms in dogs can be

either agitation or extreme quiet. Frequent urination and total unpredictability may follow. The virus paralyses the jaw and throat muscles, so that the jaw then hangs open. The dog, although thirsty, cannot swallow. If rabies is suspected, consult your vet, local doctor and police.

Ticks often attack country dogs. The sheep tick is a blood-sucking parasite, having a shiny 6mm ($\frac{1}{4}$in) long body.

The tick will be embedded in the animal, head first, so don't pull it out. Rather, dab a little ether on a pad, putting it on the tick for a couple of minutes. When the tick withdraws its head, pull it off with a pair of tweezers.

Vomiting is due to a variety of reasons, such as distemper, indigestion, overeating, nervous problems, poisoning, parasites, tumours, tonsillitis, toxaemia and hernias. If your dog continues to vomit for no apparent reason, take him along to a vet.

Worm infestations often occur during the first nine months of a dog's life. In very young animals, they produce a variety of symptoms, including a pot-belly, failure to grow normally and bad breath.

Take care that the worms are not passed to humans. Therefore, do not allow puppies to lick children's faces, and remember to wash hands before meals.

The worms can often be seen in faeces, or sometimes they are vomited. Consult your vet about the best way to free your dog of worms.

2 Working with Man

There is something magical about the way in which dogs have learnt to work in harmony with man, whether it be to shepherd or herd domestic stock or guide visually handicapped people through busy streets.

Perhaps, during the development of man from a stooping and hairy cave-dweller, the first step in the domestication of the canine race was when a dog was given shelter in return for keeping wild animals at bay. From this developed selected strains for pursuing fleet of foot wild animals, or scenting out vermin and prey, or maybe for just guarding the home.

Working dogs have always been highly prized, and it is recorded in the Ancient Welsh Laws as codified by Hywel Dda, about AD 920, that a good herding dog was worth an ox in its prime. Such is the superior strength and vigilence of the Irish Wolfhound that they were held in high esteem in Ireland, and are said to have been demanded in settlement of ransoms for nobles.

During recent years dogs with well developed scenting abilities have been used by police forces throughout the world to detect explosives and drugs. Much of this work is carried out at places of entry into a country, such as ports and airports.

The uses to which dogs have been put are many, and this chapter attempts to show how people rely on dogs to assist them to pursue their normal day-to-day activities.

Dogs for military and police use are trained with care and precision to ensure they are confident yet under the control of their handlers at all times. A dog must be able to jump from heights and to cross a variety of obstacle courses, knowing that the handler is in full control.

Above: the lithe and supple body of this German Shepherd Dog makes him an ideal police and military dog. In addition, his naturalness and high intelligence make him easily trained. His long body and gait give him an advantage when jumping over wide obstacles or streams.

Left: the Dobermann Pinscher is an alert animal which was originated in Germany by Herr Louis Dobermann in 1890. It is primarily used as a guard, police or hunting dog. It is a breed with a muscular body, and although often thought to be vicious and fierce, can be very affectionate.

Working with Man

Throughout history, man has been quick to take advantage of the natural abilities of animals for carrying goods, as fast transport or, like pigeons, as message carriers. It is, therefore, quite natural that dogs should have been put to the wide range of activities they perform for man, from guarding flocks and herds to hunting truffles, as guide dogs for blind people and as protectors of our freedom when used in police forces.

Police Dogs

There are few police forces in the world that do not use dogs in the tracking and apprehension of criminals, and their activities have even extended to detecting drugs and explosives by the distinctive scents they emit. In addition, dogs are used just to give weight to the police, as few villains would wish to tackle a trained police dog.

Several different breeds are in use with the police, the specific type depending on the work they are put to. For instance, Labradors are frequently used in dock areas and at airports to detect drugs, while the more active and lithe dogs such as German Shepherd Dogs and Dobermann Pinschers are involved in the apprehension of criminals.

The training of these dogs is long and thorough, and only the animals attaining a high standard are used. They have to be fearless at all times, to temper their aggression and instantly act on words and signals of command.

Most of the dogs used by the police are described within other chapters, but the Dobermann Pinscher is unique. His origin is relatively recent, and was created in Germany by Herr Louis Dobermann of Apolda, Thuringia, just before the turn of the century. This is a dog formed from several breeds, including the Black-and-tan Terrier, Rottweiler and German Pinscher. The outcome of these crosses is a most able and intelligent dog, with a short coat needing little attention.

This is a breed that is best suited as a one-man dog. Although they are usually docile and affectionate, some strains are very quick to attack.

In color they can be black, brown, or blue with tan markings.

Dogs for the Blind

Everyone who has seen a guide dog in action, carefully guiding a visually handicapped person through busy streets, cannot fail to be impressed by the skill, good temper and understanding of these treasured animals. Without them, many people could not carry on a daily existence of travel, work, shopping, or just visiting friends.

The first use of dogs as guides for blind people began after the First World War in Germany, when each war-blinded soldier was introduced to a trained dog which could act as a guide. So successful was this, that the idea rapidly spread to Switzerland, France and Italy. A school was set up in Switzerland at Vevey, becoming the most well-known establishment for the training of dogs for civilians.

During 1930, the idea of guide dogs for the blind spread to Britain, and at Wal-

lasey, in Cheshire, the Guide Dog for the Blind Association was founded.

This great humanitarian cause has now spread throughout the world, and frequently such dogs as Labradors, German Shepherd Dogs, Boxers and Dobermann Pinschers are used. However, the breed most often utilized is the German Shepherd Dog, as he is very responsive during training, of a good temperament and trustworthy.

Only bitches are normally used, as they are not so distracted by other dogs and are less likely to wander off. Bitches normally have a more responsible attitude than dogs and are generally more receptive to training. However, castrated dogs have been used quite successfully.

The guide dog wears a special harness which enables the blind person to have control of the animal and to feel every movement of the dog. Although each dog is under the control of the handler, they nevertheless display a great deal of their own initiative.

Most of the dogs used as guides are described in this and other chapters, except for the Boxer, which despite its playful character, makes an ideal guide and companion.

Boxers This is a distinctive and very handsome dog. His origin is not certain, and is thought to be a cross between an English Bulldog and a Great Dane. As such, it is believed that he was originated

to fight wild boars and to bait bulls. Indeed, this is substantiated by the fact that the word boxer is possibly a corruption of the German word *Beisser*, or biter.

Although they look aggressive, they are usually playful and lively, with a controlled temper. However, they are subject to tantrums. They are also inclined to snore and drip saliva over the floor and carpets. Notwithstanding this, they make faithful friends and tend to be easily trained.

Draft Dogs

These dogs, of course, are heavier and more muscular than those breeds used for herding or shepherding other animals. Furthermore, draft dogs in temperate climes differ markedly from those in colder areas. It is dogs of the Spitz group, the Huskies, that work in cold climates and are used to haul sledges, and these are discussed later in this chapter.

At one time, draft dogs were used extensively throughout Europe, hauling small carts carrying such goods as milk, cheeses, eggs, bread and farm produce. It has been said that at one time there were 175,000 dogs in Belgium alone, and were used to pull carts for tradesmen such as bakers and grocers. Before 1839 draft dogs were used in England, but such was the row from their incessant barking that they were banned from the highways.

Most of these working dogs were well cared for by their owners, and admirably protected from abuse by local bye-laws. This is especially so of Belgium and Switzerland, where extensive trouble was taken to ensure that the dogs were fit, the loads not too heavy and harnesses fitted the animals.

The inspection of the dogs and carts could take place at any time, and the dogs were especially checked for sores where the harness touched the body. The feet were checked for disorders, and if necessary the dogs were made to wear leather or rubber bootees until they recovered fitness. In cold weather, protective dog coats were worn, and in Italy the animals were compelled to rest and even shaded from strong sunlight.

Many different breeds have been used as draft dogs, and a few of them are described in the following pages.

Bernese Mountain Dog Often known as the Berner Sennenhund, this type of Swiss Mountain Dog has a long coat, making him a very handsome fellow.

He was used to haul carts holding dairy and bakery produce.

The breed was introduced into Britain during 1936, and in 1937 was admitted into the American Kennel Club. It is a breed with a long, soft and silky coat, thick all over the body.

Leonberg Sometimes called the Leonberger or Leonburg, this handsome draft dog was bred by Herr Essig of

Above: huskies and a sledge are the key to travel in the snow-covered world of the arctic and antarctic. No other breed has the fortitude and resistance to cold as the husky, who remains loyal through sub-zero conditions. The term Husky means a sledge dog, and many canine authorities suggest that only above the 55th parallel do real huskies exist. Below that line, the sledge hauling dogs are weaker and a mixture of other breeds.

Above left: the Newfoundland is a water dog in his native country. He has a gentle and pleasing disposition, making him an excellent pet for children. For many years he was used to haul small carts and retrieve fishing gear lost overboard from fishing boats.

Leonburg, in Württemberg on the Bavarian border in about 1850, and first exhibited in Britain during 1948.

Within his ancestry are the Newfoundland, St. Bernard, the Old Wallis Sheepdog and, possibly, the Bernese Mountain Dog.

It was not until 1875 that the breed was considered to be settled, when it was accepted as a pure breed at an exhibition in Berlin as well as in Württemberg.

In Flanders the dog was used to haul small carts carrying bread, milk and grocery products.

Newfoundland This handsome dog has a long association with the country of that name, although it cannot be proven that the breed originated there. However, for many years he was used to pull fishermen's carts laden with fuel. He is an

excellent swimmer, and used on many occasions to retrieve fishing equipment lost overboard.

About the middle of the eighteenth century he was introduced into Britain, and a variation of the breed became famous when he was painted by Sir Edwin Landseer.

A few years ago the breed was becoming scarce in Newfoundland, but has found renewed interest throughout Canada and the United States of America. In color, the popular Newfoundland is a dull jet black, while the Landseer Newfoundland is black-and-white particolored.

Swiss Mountain Dog The Large Swiss Mountain Dog, or Grosse Schweizer Sennenhund, is the largest of the Swiss Mountain Dogs. He is a dog that led a

Left: the world-famous St. Bernard probably arrived in Britain about the beginning of the nineteenth century. Like the Landseer Newfoundland, this breed was also made famous through the paintings of Sir Edwin Landseer. During 1815, the British St. Bernard club was formed, and in 1884 the Swiss St. Bernard club was started, and this led to the increased popularity of the breed.

Far left: sledge-hauling dogs have a noble past, being used by the Royal Canadian Mounted Police, trappers, Eskimos, Indians, traders, doctors and priests. The coats of these dogs are intensely dense, with a very thick undercoat. Their eyes are dark and set obliquely, so as to protect them from strong light reflected off the ice. The set of the eyes also offers protection from penetrating wind.

Left, below: the Landseer Newfoundland was made famous by Sir Edwin Landseer, who depicted this attractive dog in many paintings.

dual role, hauling small vehicles for dairy and vegetable farmers and guarding and protecting flocks and herds. About the turn of the last century, the breed was on the verge of extinction, but thanks to dedicated dog breeders in Switzerland, and especially Professor Albert Heim of Zürich, the breed was re-established and a pure bred specimen was exhibited in 1908.

Sledge Dogs
These are some of the hardiest of all dogs, able to survive sub-zero temperatures that would kill other members of the canine race. These dogs are of the Spitz group, which includes such breeds as the Chow Chow (Chinese Spitz), the Elkhound, Husky, Karelian Bjornhund (Bear-hunting dog of Karelia), Keeshond (Dutch Spitz), Samoyed (Spitz of Siberia), Schipperke (Belgian Barge or Canal Dog), and Vallhund (Swedish cattle-herding Spitz).

The Husky epitomizes the sledge dog. However, there are various types of Husky, depending on the area in which they are used.

To haul the sledges, several different types of hitch are used. The traditional hitch is the fan, in which each dog is attached individually to the sledge. Between twelve and fifteen dogs are used to each sledge, and any dog not pulling his weight can easily be seen and the culprit dealt with rapidly. This type of hitch is often used by the Eskimos and Indians of the eastern and northern areas of North America. It is an especially good hitch where the trail is wide and flat, as the leads to each dog can be up to 18m (60ft) long, but usually 6-9m (20-30ft).

Another hitch is the double Indian file, where two dogs are hitched in pairs behind each other. Often known as the

Right: the Dalmatian is one of the clowns of the dog world. He has been known as the 'plum pudding dog', 'spotted dick' and 'fire house dog' during his career as a war dog, ratter, shepherd, sporting hound and a protector of stage coaches. He is one of the most friendly dogs in the world, with a disposition that endears him to everyone he meets.

Far right: this Samoyed is a member of the Spitz group. He is known as the Spitz of Siberia, and is perhaps one of the most handsome of all dogs working in cold climates. He gains his name from the Samoyed tribe who live on the northern edge of the Siberian Plain. This breed is well known in the colder parts of the United States of America.

Far right below: this Newfoundland loves the water, from which he will readily retrieve sticks.

'two-by-two', 'gang' or 'pair' hitch, it is difficult to know if each dog is pulling well. Between six and sixteen dogs are used to each sledge, but usually the number is eight.

In Russia, six dogs are often used, in two rows, three abreast. And in some parts of North America three or four dogs are used in a single line when hauling light loads.

True sledge dogs are easily recognized. They have a broad skull, with a sharp and pointed muzzle. The ears are relatively small, but erect, and the body is square and powerful with a coat of hair that is abundant all over the body.

Husky This name is used for a wide variety of dogs, and indeed the name Husky means 'sledge dog'. However, not all sledge dogs are huskies, as many cross-breeds are used. It is generally said that all dogs above the 55th parallel are more like the true husky, being a lot hardier than the sledge dogs used below that latitude.

Samoyed This is the Spitz of Siberia, and perhaps the most handsome working dog used in the Arctic Circle. It gains its name from the nomadic Samoyed tribe who lived on the northern edge of the Siberian Plain. It is a multi-purpose breed, and is

equally at home as a herder or guard dog as well as hauling a sledge.

The Samoyed is typical of the Spitz group, with a ruff of long hair around the neck, and a lovely white or white-and-biscuit and cream coat which hangs generously all over the body.

Search and Rescue Dogs

There are a few dogs that are world famous, but perhaps none more so than the St. Bernard. What better known rescue dog can there be?

He gains his name from the monk Bernard de Menthon and the Hospice of the St. Bernard Pass in the Swiss Alps. The breed is first mentioned in 1774, in the records of the Hospice, but canine experts suggest that he was known in 1665 when monks trained them to search for people lost in the valley.

The breed was popularized in England by the British-born painter Sir Edwin Landseer who depicted one of this noble breed fighting his way through a snow storm to reach a lost traveler.

He is one of the most lovable and devoted family dogs one could ever wish to have, and is very loyal. In color he may be white with red, or red with white, with a white chest, feet and tail tip.

Fishing Dogs

Although there are several dogs which help fishermen to guard their nets and catches, such as the Newfoundland and the New Guinea Native Dog, which will retrieve escaping fish, the most well known fishing dog is the Portuguese Water Dog. This distinctive fellow, also known as the Portuguese Fishing dog or Cao d'Agua, is an exceptional swimmer and diver, and is used by the native fishermen to dive and locate broken fishing nets and to recapture fish which have escaped from a hook. He is even employed as a courier of messages between boats, and from boats to the shore.

There are two varieties of this breed; the popular Long-coated Portuguese Water Dog and the Curly-coated Portuguese Water Dog. The two dogs are basically the same, but the coat of the curly type is short and formed of tight curls, much like those of the Irish Water Spaniel. The breed is able to swim considerable distances when delivering messages.

Truffle Dogs

The much sought after truffle is an underground fungi of the *Ascomycetes* family, and relished by gourmets the world over and particularly in France

Indeed, the French at one time hunted the truffle with pigs which were specially trained to scent out these edible fungi.

The truffle is seasonal between September and the end of February, and can be found just under the soil surface in woods of oak, beech, poplar, hazel, elm, willow and lime trees. All truffle dogs need sensitive noses if they are to be successful. Many breeds have been used, including the Bassett Hound and dogs of the Poodle type called 'Truffleurs'. Good dogs can detect truffles at 110m (100yd) if they are in light soil and not more than 7.5cm (3in) deep.

Guard Dogs

These are dogs which in size range from the diminutive Lhasa Apso to the Great Dane, and can guard either by barking and drawing attention to invaders or by a fearsome nature and large appearance. There are, of course, many guard dogs, but some of the more usual ones warrant a mention.

Dalmatian No-one who has ever seen this dog will ever forget him. Originally he was a sporting dog, but was used in France during the seventeenth century to protect coachers from robbers.

In his time he has also been a war dog, a ratter, a shepherd dog, a sporting dog, as well as a fine house dog.

He is a sturdy fellow, intelligent and with a disposition that enables him to make friends very easily. In color he is pure white with distinctive black or dark brown spots. His coat is fine, glossy, hard and dense.

Keeshond This is the Dutch Barge Hound, and during the heyday of commercial barging he was to be seen on most barges in Holland, acting as a guard dog. This is a dog, by the way, that gains his name from Kees de Glyselaer, a leader of a nationalistic Dutch political party during the mid-eighteenth century. Indeed, the Keeshond is a well-known dog throughout the Low-countries and Holland.

He is a tough and resiliant dog, cool and polite to strangers, but untrusting towards them. He is essentially a one-man dog. In color he is wolf and ash-gray, with a long and straight coat.

Lhasa Apso This is supposed to be a lucky dog, bringing good fortune to his owner. This breed, also known as the Tibetan Apso and the Barking Sentinel Lion Dog, has been known for well over 800 years. Such is his fame, that from the

Above: the Lhasa Apso from Tibet has been known for more than 800 years, and is also called the Tibetan Apso and Abso Seng Kye — the Bark Sentinel Lion Dog. Ownership of this attractive dog is thought to bring good luck. For many years they were given as presents from the Dalai Lama of Tibet to dignitaries all over the world.

Right: dogs have been utilized in war for many centuries. At first they were large and fearsome creatures who were used to frighten invaders. As the means of waging war became more sophisticated messenger dogs were needed, and alert and intelligent breeds such as the German Shepherd Dog were used. This illustration shows a dog being used during the American involvement in the Vietnam war. A scout dog called 'Kelly' of the 38th dog platoon awaits the word of command beside a soldier.

sixteenth century and until the turn of this century the Dalai Lama of Tibet gave treasured presents of this dog to high dignitaries in China.

The word Apso means goat-like and this is very apt for this small and heavily coated dog. In his native Tibet he was used to guard monasteries.

Schipperke This is the Belgian Barge Dog, and can be traced back to the sixteenth century and the Flemish provinces of Belgium. He has the typical appearance of the Spitz group, and although small makes a vigilant protector of property.

He is probably the hardiest of all the small dogs and is quite fearless, with a most aggressive bark. At one time he was used to protect barges in Belgium, and became very popular when in 1885

Queen Marie Henriette of Belgium had one as a pet.

He is black in color, with an abundant coat often having a harsh appearance.

Dogs in War

It probably did not take man long to appreciate the fearsome and aggressive value in dogs. The exact date when early man set his cur on his neighbor in settlement of inter-tribal brawls is unknown. Albeit to say that dogs were then specially selected for their ferocity and ugly nature. The cultured Romans were so impressed with the fighting dogs of the Ancient Britons when they invaded Britain that they took them back to Rome to fight in arenas against lions, bulls and bears.

During the two World Wars of

1914-1918 and 1939-1945, dogs were used to carry messages through dangerous areas. They were even used by the Americans during their involvement in the Vietnam War.

Pastoral Dogs

Without these trusty and alert dogs, it is true to say that much of the commercial life during the past hundreds of years would not have been possible. Without the ability to protect and control vast flocks of sheep, little industrial weaving could have been achieved. And without the cattle-herding dogs, the rapid expansion of population, which in its turn fed the industrial revolution, would not have been possible.

Many of the herding and shepherding dogs are discussed in Chapter Four.

Sporting Gun Dogs

The unique relationship between man and dog make them ideal partners when shooting and recovering game. The dog so obviously wants to please his master, and the man is quite happy to let the dog chase miles over the countryside to recover a shot game bird.

Gun dogs need to be highly intelligent, have good eyesight, a keen sense of smell, and to be fleet enough of foot to recover game quickly. Of course, they do not have to run fast enough to overtake prey, but just scent out and return the shot game to their master.

The selection and development of gun dogs has closely followed the refinement and increasing sophistication of guns. With the inception of the muzzle-loading firing piece came the development of the Pointer, able to indicate through keen senses of smell and hearing the direction of the game. Later, the Setters were developed.

Gun dogs, such as Pointers, Setters, Retrievers and Spaniels, are some of the best family dogs, all of which are tolerant of small children. These animals are a delight to train, but still manage to exhibit a great deal of character and playfulness which endears them to everyone they meet.

These gun dogs are about to embark on a shoot in the country. They include dogs such as setters, retrievers, pointers and spaniels, who love the company of man and the excitement of this sport. The training of these dogs takes a long time, and an experienced gun dog is very valuable to his owner.

Above: the Red Setter is one of the happiest of all dogs. His coat is a glorious rich chestnut with no trace of black. In the late 1860s he was imported into the United States of America as a bird dog.

Left: this English Setter is one of the most handsome and stately of the setters, with a proud head and charming disposition. His lineage can be traced back several centuries to the days of Queen Elizabeth the First. He is good natured, with few rivals in the show ring.

Sporting Gun Dogs

These are some of the most attractive of all dogs, as well as displaying a high degree of devotion and loyalty.

Setters

The Setter group are so called because they were originally trained in crouching or 'setting' at the sight of the game they were to pursue. The term setting, by the way, means to sit. Originally, their purpose was to creep low through cover, driving the game into nets. However, with the advent of shooting birds on the wing, their role has turned to be one of the all-purpose gun dog.

English Setter This is a very handsome breed that has been in sport for hundreds of years. Indeed, he was mentioned by Johannes Caius — Queen Elizabeth the First's Physician-in-chief — in 1570 in his book *De Canibus Britannicis*.

This intensely friendly and good natured dog has few equals as a show animal. His coat may be colored either black-and-white, lemon-and-white, liver-and-white, or tricolor.

German Setters There are two types of this attractive breed: the Grosser Münsterländer (the larger Setter), which is native to Münster and black-and-white with generous feathers and the Kleiner Münsterländer (the smaller Setter). He is colored brown-and-white.

Gordon Setter This is a distinctive and stylish dog with a 'galloping' line, which was first heard of at Gordon Castle in Banffshire, Scotland. The Gordon Setter Club was founded in 1927, and since then he has become very popular.

His coat should be soft and shining, with long hair on his ears. The color of his coat is a deep shining coal-black with tan markings, either of a rich chestnut or a mahogany red.

Irish Setter Few dogs can be so distinctive as this attractive breed, which is so often called the Red Setter. His glorious coat is a rich chestnut with no trace of black. His distinctive gait and mischievious look endear him to many families.

Pointers

The hardy and active pointers need plenty of exercise, when they are ideal for hunting, pointing and retrieving. They gain their name from the stance they adopt when scenting game birds — the head and tail stretches out. The pointer has been known for over 200 years, and was listed in the Gmelin-Kerr edition of *The Animal Kingdom* in 1792.

Pointer He has a handsome appearance with a clean-cut look, having a fine, short and hard evenly distributed coat. The usual colors are lemon-and-white, orange-and-white, liver-and-white and black-and-white.

German Pointer The German Short-haired Pointer is often considered to be a superb dual-purpose dog, being both an excellent pointer and retriever. He has a

very keen nose and great perseverance when searching out game, and is equally good on land or in water.

He is a very noble and steady dog, with a coat which may be of various colors: solid liver, liver-and-white spotted, liver-and-white spotted and ticked, and liver-and-white ticked.

Retrievers

Retrievers are widely acclaimed for their gentle disposition, making them excellent as retrievers of game birds. They are also ideal as family pets, being very tolerant of young children.

Chesapeake Bay Retriever This is a famous and popular American gundog, mainly used in the shooting of duck along the Eastern Seaboard. His coat is rather short, but wavy, and colored anything from red sedge to dark tan. His speciality is said to be retrieving wildfowl from water. In such circumstances, his remarkably oily coat enables him to shed water and ice just by shaking his body.

Curly-coated Retriever This is one of the oldest British gundogs, with a smart, strong and upstanding manner. His coat, which is black or liver, is formed by masses of short, tight crisp curls. Although difficult to prove, it is thought that he is related through his ancestry to the Poodle and the Irish Water Spaniel. He has great determination when retrieving game, especially from water, and is a delightful work dog and companion.

His fame extends throughout the world, and in New Zealand and Australia is particularly famous for retrieving game such as quail and duck.

Flat-coated Retriever He is an alert, bright and active dog with an intelligent expression. Formerly he was called the 'wavy-coated' retriever, until a cross with the Collies was used, making his coat flatter and more resistant to the penetration of water. Other breeds which have been used in his development are the Newfoundland, Setters and Labrador.

He has a keen nose, a faithful heart, and is superb with children, displaying a natural warmth. His coat is black or liver

Above: this English Springer Spaniel is majestic in appearance, as well as being a superb family dog. He loves children, allowing them to pull him about. He also makes a good watchdog. Originally he was trained as a field dog to retrieve duck.

Above: originally, the Pointer was a continental dog, but it was the English who developed the animal we know today. The early Pointers were used to locate and chase hares. He is certainly not a dog for city life, as he needs plenty of exercise and open country.

in color, and dense and flat.

Golden Retriever He is a handsome dog, and is perhaps one of the best hunting dogs, displaying all the abilities of the Setters and Retrievers, and at the same time being able to follow a scent as keenly as a Bloodhound. His coat is an attractive rich golden color, the texture being dense and water resistant. For a good family dog there are few that excel him for worthiness, friendliness, loyalty and trust.

Labrador Retriever This is a strongly built dog, with a black, short, dense coat without the trace of a wave. His weather-resistant undercoat should be fairly hard. It is thought that this attractive dog first came to England through Poole Harbour, in Dorset, in about 1840, in ships trading from Labrador.

As a companion he has great charm,

being gracious, even tempered and very loyal.

There is a yellow-coated type, which may vary in color from fox-red to cream, without any white on the chest or tips of the toes. It is often incorrectly referred to as the Golden Labrador.

Spaniels

Spaniels are delightful dogs with distinctive personalities. They make excellent family animals, being loyal, gentle, docile and affectionate. In the field, they are used for starting and retrieving game.

Clumber Spaniel He is easily trained for field work, but tends to be slower than the Springers. It is a breed that dates back to 1790, taking his name from 'Clumber', the seat of the Duke of Newcastle. He also makes a good guard dog, but often produces plenty of fat if not exercised frequently. Although popular as a companion in the Edwardian era, his popularity has waned during recent years.

His coat is plain white, with lemon markings. Orange markings are permissible, but not desirable.

Cocker Spaniel One of the most popular of the spaniel family, combining an appealing manner with brains and beauty. He derives his name from his ability to flush out woodcock from areas inaccessible to other spaniels. His ancestry goes back well over 200 years, and during recent years has become very popular as a family pet.

His coat is flat and silky in texture, but never wiry or wavy. Cockers can be of many colours, but usually blue or red roan, red, golden, black, parti-coloured or liver. He should be well feathered, particularly on the ears.

Field Spaniel This is a British breed and a close relative of the Cocker. Indeed, it is said to have been bred for field work from the Sussex and Cocker spaniels. He is now chiefly kept as a family pet — not having the 'doggy' smell that so many families object to.

His coat is slightly waved or flat, but never curled. He is usually black, but can be black-and-tan, or liver.

Irish Water Spaniel This good all-round dog is said to be a cross between the Northern Irish Water Spaniel and the Southern Irish Water Spaniel. With his peculiar gait, he differs from all other spaniels.

He was bred for all types of shooting, but is particularly suited to wildfowling. He is a distinctive fellow, with a coat formed of dense, tight, crisp ringlets, and coloured a rich, dark liver, with a purplish tint or bloom. He is often thought to be the clown of the spaniel family.

English Springer Spaniel He is the oldest of the sporting gundogs, and is said to be the ancestor of all the sporting land spaniels, with exception of the Clumber. Originally, he was used for finding and springing game to the net, but is now used to find, flush and retrieve game.

He is a merry and active dog, built for endurance and activity. His coat should be close, straight and weather resistant. In colour, he is normally liver-and-white or black-and-white, or these colours with tan markings. At one time he used to be called the Norfolk Spaniel.

Sussex Spaniel He is a massive and muscular dog, but with a lively and free action. Originally he was bred as a tough

Above: this Kleiner Münsterlander, the smaller of the German Setters, is coloured brown-and-white. The larger German Setter is black-and-white, with generous feathers. They are gentle dogs, making good pets for homes with children.

Right: it is essential that all gun dogs behave properly and respond quickly to words of command. This German Pointer is watchful of his master, who is preparing for the shoot. Gun dogs who rush out of control are quite likely to be shot accidentally.

and short-legged dog for flushing game from the thick hedgerows of Sussex. He has an abundant body coat which is flat, with no tendency to curl, and colored a rich golden liver.

Welsh Springer Spaniel This is a very ancient breed, and said to be the only Spaniel native to Wales. He is thought to be a progeny of a race mentioned in the Ancient Laws of Wales, and codified by Hywel Dda, Howell the good King of Wales, about AD 900. With his straight or flat thick coat of a silky texture, he is a very attractive fellow. The color of his coat is a dark, rich red or white.

Other Breeds

Vizsla This is an all-purpose gundog which originated in Hungary. He is able to mark the fall of a bird, and to retrieve it on command. It is an ancient breed, and often called the Hungarian Yellow Pointer. In height he is about 63cm (25in) at the shoulder, with a sedge-yellow, short and smooth coat.

Vorstehhund These German gundogs are very distinctive. There are three types, but only two are really popular. The Kurzhaariger is short-haired and used both as a gundog and show dog. His color is variable and includes chestnut, chestnut-and-white, and red roan. The second most popular is the Langhaariger, which is basically a short-tailed Pointer with a flat and long coat.

Weimaraner This is an exceptionally alert and attractive dog, originating from Weimar, East Germany. Originally he was employed to track game, although now he is used to point and retrieve. However, he is such an excellent dog, that he is used by many police forces, where his alertness and obedience are used to the full. He is well known throughout the United States of America.

He is a dog with the attractive nickname of 'gray ghost', which relates to his distinctive silvery gray color. His eyes take on a very piercing quality, being a yellowish hazel shade.

Chapter 4 Pastoral Dogs

Dogs have been used since time immemorial to herd sheep and cattle, playing a unique role in assisting man to control and protect his stock. Without these dogs, it would have been impossible for man to look after such large flocks and herds, and to many people and countries this could have meant economic disaster.

Pastoral dogs are some of the most intelligent animals in the world, and include in their ranks animals of all sizes. For instance, the diminutive Shetland Sheepdog is but 30cm (12in)high at the shoulder, whereas the Russian Sheepdog, the Owtcharka, is over 75cm (30in). Furthermore, these pastoral dogs are extremely variable in their coats. The Rough-coated Collie has an attractive covering of long and soft hair, while the Puli, which comes from Hungary, has a coat of long and very dense tangled mats.

The differences between pastoral dogs are numerous, and result from their use and the part of the world in which they live. It is logical to expect this variation, but there are several things which they all have in common, such as an even temperament when dealing with other animals, a high degree of intelligence and keen sight.

Pastoral dogs must also have the temperament to live in harmony with their masters, as well as with sheep or cattle. They must have a lasting sense of duty, especially in extremes of weather when lesser dogs would not survive.

Without a high intelligence, these working dogs would soon be killed. They have to be able to outwit and think marauding animals, act quickly on words and whistles of command, avoid difficult natural hazards such as cliffs and ravines, as well as having to be aware of mechanical equipment used nowadays on farms.

The Bob-tail Sheepdog, or Old English Sheepdog as he is often called, is perhaps the most well known of all pastoral dogs. He has a charming disposition, making friends with everyone he meets. These dogs are inclined to demand a great deal of attention, often taking on the role of another child in the family. They walk with a bounce that gives them an air of superiority and confidence.

Above: the Briard is a French sheepdog whose ancestors date back to the twelfth century. His home district in France is Brie, and it is recorded that Charlemagne gave braces of them as presents. It is a breed that is well known in the United States of America, especially in the New England area. He was introduced into America in 1927, and was soon recognized by the American Kennel Club.

Left: the Rough-coated Collie is one of the most intelligent and attractive sheepdogs. The head of this dog radiates assuredness and confidence. Indeed, the whole dog is beautifully proportioned, giving the stamina required for pastoral duties as well as the speed needed to pursue sheep over great distances.

Pastoral Dogs

Anyone who has been fortunate enough to see a sheepdog at work, tirelessly running from one side of a flock to another, at the word or whistle of command, will never forget the sight.

In order to use their intelligence to the full, these dogs have to be able to receive signals quickly and easily, whether they be visual, as a sound, or through a scent in the air. Usually, these dogs have equally good eyesight, keenness of nose and a sensitive ear.

It is impossible in a book of this size to include all of the pastoral dogs in the world, and therefore a selection has been made to show their vast range.

Apenzell Mountain Dog This is a small and popular Swiss mountain dog, a hardy breed and used for herding sheep and driving cattle. He has a thick, short-haired glossy coat, colored jet black with brown and white markings.

Armant An Egyptian sheep dog with a fierce disposition. Although little known in Britain, he was introduced to Britain by an Egyptian Minister to the Court of St. James. His coat is rather shaggy, and in many ways he resembles an Old English Sheepdog. In color he may be black,

black-and-tan, black-and-white, tan-and white, tri-colored or grizzle-and-white.

Australian Heeler This comparatively recent breed, also known as the Australian Cattle Dog, has a number of breeds in his ancestry, including the Dingo, which is the Australian Wild Dog, the Kelpie, also known as the Australian Sheepdog, Collie and Dalmatian.

He is an excellent and hardy dog, running in and around cattle and herding by nipping their heels. His coat is short, hard in texture and close lying. In color his coat may be red-speckled or blue-speckled, red-and-tan and even red-and-white.

The *Barb* The Barb is another superb Australian sheep dog. He is often confused with the Kelpie, which is somewhat shorter. His body is muscular and square, with rather long legs. His coat is short, but around the neck the hair is longer, something he inherits from his Collie ancestry. He is black in color.

Bouvier des Ardennes A long established cattle dog of the Belgian Ardennes. Although his ancestry is not clear, it is thought that he is descended from the Bouvier de Flandres, the Belgian Malinois

Right: the Entlebuch Sennenhund, often known as the Entlebuch Mountain Dog, is a native of Switzerland. At one time this distinctive breed was near extinction, but since the Thirties has prospered.

Far right: the German Shepherd Dog can trace his origin back many years — a German expert of this breed traced it back to the Early Bronze Age, about 6,000 years ago. It is a breed that gained the name, quite incorrectly, Alsatian, after the Alsace region from whence it was introduced into Britain. In his native country he is called Deutscher Schäferhund, which translates to German Shepherd Dog. In France he is known as Chien de Berger Allemagne, and in Spain Perro de Pastor Alleman.

and the Briard, the French Sheepdog.

This Ardennes dog is a capable worker and deserves to be better known. His body is rather square, with a deep chest and muscular loins. The coat is relatively short on the head and legs, and medium in length on the rest of his body, making him appear rather shaggy. He is black or light gray in color.

Bouvier de Flandres This is one of the most used and popular cattle dogs in the Low Countries. In appearance he is like the Giant Schnauzer: square cobby and rugged. His coat is short to medium, looking rather shaggy. In color he can be quite black, or dark gray.

Briard Also known as the Chien de Berger de Brie — from the same area as the delicious cheese of that name — this native of France has a lineage which can be traced back to the twelfth century, and it is claimed that Charlemagne gave braces of them as presents to his friends. Napoleon is also known to have liked this breed and to have taken them with him on expeditions to Egypt. The breed was introduced into the United States of America in 1927, and is known throughout the area of New England.

There are two distinct types: the Woolly-haired and the Smooth-haired. The Woolly-haired is the most popular, with a medium to long coat, slightly wavy but not curled. With the smooth type, the coat lies close to the skin and is of medium length and glossy.

Catalan Sheepdog A rather handsome Spanish sheep and cattle dog. In Catalonia this breed is called Perro de Pastor Catalán, and in Spain, Gos d'Atura. There are two varieties of this breed, the long-haired and short-haired. During the Spanish Civil War they were used to carry despatches with great tenacity and courage.

Collie This is a world-famous breed, and owes the name Collie to the Colley Dog, which was used to shepherd the Scottish native mountain sheep called colleys. However, the names Colley Dog and Scotch Dog have now become obsolete. There are three types of Collies: Rough-coated, Smooth-coated, and the Bearded Collie.

The Rough-coated Collie tends to be the most popular, having an exceptionally high intelligence. He is a beautiful dog, with a clear expression and wonderful carriage. He has an abundant coat, mane and frill, and makes a most devoted and faithful friend. In color he may be sable-and-white, blue merle, or black with tan-and-white markings.

The Smooth-coated type differs only in his coat, which should be dense, hard and smooth.

The Bearded Collie, however, is quite different and one of the oldest British sheepdogs, which at one time was becoming rare. He is square set, and nearly as heavy as the Old English Sheepdog. His coat is long and shaggy,

and abundant all over his body. He has had many names in his life, including Highland Collie, Mountain Collie and Hairy Mou'ed Collie.

Cumberland Sheepdog This north of England dog is well known in Westmorland, Cumberland and the Peak District. It is a dog bred by the late Lord Lonsdale, who, at one time, it is said, had more than thirty of these wonderfully sagacious animals.

In appearance, the Cumberland Sheepdog looks very much like a combination of the working collie and Welsh Sheepdog, being distinctively lithe. His coat is long, dense and black, with a white blaze on the chest, and white on the legs feet and tip of the tail.

Dutch Herder This is the national breed of Holland, where he is known as the Nederlandsche Herdershonden. He is an ancient breed, and has spread to Australia, where he was recorded several hundred years ago. Although his origins are rather obscure, it is thought that the German Shepherd Dog and the Giant Schnauzer played a part in his lineage.

There are three distinct types of this breed: Rough-coated, Long-coated and the Smooth-coated, but apart from the length and texture of coat, they are all alike.

The head of the Dutch Herder looks like a combination of the Malinois and the Giant Schnauzer. The most common color is gray, but dark brindle, iron-gray,

steel-gray, blue-gray, cinder-gray and silver-gray are known. White and any of the pied mixtures are not acceptable.

Entlebuch Mountain Dog This is the smallest of the Swiss Mountain dogs, and often known as the Entlebucher Sennenhund, deriving his name from a river which flows through the Canton of Lucerne. At one time the breed neared extinction, but since the 1930s interest has revived in them.

He has a smooth short coat which is extra soft on the head and face. In color he is white-and-tan-and-black.

German Shepherd Dog Perhaps no other dog is so distinctive and world famous for his expression of constant alertness and perpetual vigilance. He is alive to every sound and movement and has a high degree of intelligence. The breed gained the name Alsatian Wolfdog in 1919, and was introduced into Britain during the beginning of this century as the German Sheepdog.

This breed's origins can be traced back many centuries, and the late Captain Max von Stephanitz, a renowned authority on this dog, suggested that the race dated back to the Early Bronze Age something like 6,000 years ago. It is a dog whose size, alertness and peculiar loping gait when running is known to all. The coat is generally short, but longer on the flanks and back. In color the breed may be sable, wolf-gray, brindle and black-and-tan, silver-gray, all black or all white.

Groenendael This is a Belgian dog which takes its name from a small village near Brussels, and has been recognized in Belgium as a pure breed since 1891. During the First World War they were used by the Belgian Army for carrying messages. They were also used to find and aid wounded soldiers in no-man's land. In appearance he is very much like the German Shepherd Dog. However, his body coat is generally long, but short on the face, and in color black all over or with a little white on the cheek and muzzle.

Icelandic Sheepdog This breed has been mentioned in various books, including *De Canibus Britannicis* by Dr. Caius in 1570 and by Carl von Linné, who, two centuries later, referred to him as *Canis Islandicus*, or Iceland Dog. His coat is short on the face and the front of his legs, but long on the neck, back and hindquarters. The color is generally black, or black with white or gray on the chest, feet and tip of the tail.

Above: one variation in color for the German Shepherd Dog is black, making a very distinctive animal of ferocious countenance. He is a handsome dog. Other colors may be sable, wolf-gray, brindle and black-and-tan, silvery-gray, and all white.

Right: the Kuvasz is a noble breed from Hungary. At one time he was used for shepherd duties on the Hungarian steppes. The breed takes its name from the Turkish 'Kawasz', meaning 'Guardian of the Nobles'. It is a handsome animal, and well-known in America.

Illyrian Sheepdog This is a typical Croatian dog, from the northern ranges of the Illyrian mountains, and has been officially recognized by the canine governing body of Yugoslavia. It is a breed that has been used to herd sheep and goats, as well as cattle.

In color his coat is usually sable, but other popular colors are wolf-gray, light brindle with cream or white throat, feet and tail plume, and black-and-tan.

Kelpie Also known as the Australian Sheepdog, this attractive Australian sheepdog is thought to have been developed from dogs taken to that continent by old Scottish and Welsh settlers. The modern Kelpie is the result of careful selection, but legend has the derivation of the breed as a crossing between a bitch cross-bred Dingo/Collie named 'Kelpie' which was crossed with a Collie named 'Caesar' and resulted in a black-and-tan bitch so resembling its dam that it was called 'Kelpie II'.

'Kelpie II' won the first Australian Sheepdog Trials held at Forbes, New South Wales, about one hundred years ago, and was the foundation stock for all Kelpies.

The Kelpie is an excellent sheepherder, being conscientious and well able to handle several thousand sheep. He has a short and harsh coat, often a little longer on the neck. In color the coat is black-and-tan, blue-and-tan, red-and-tan, red, blue, chocolate or fawn.

Komondor An attractive animal and one of the oldest of the European dogs, originating in Tibet and entering Europe with the Magyar invaders about 1,000 years ago. He is a distinctive fellow, with long, dense, soft, woolly white hair entangled and shaggy.

Kuvasz This is another old Hungarian breed, arriving with the great Magyar migration. By the fifteenth century he had become popular with nobility, and in 1458 was bred by King Matthias. The dog's name, incidentally, is not Hungarian but Turkish, and means 'Guardian of Nobles'.

The breed is an excellent guardian of farm animals, being exceptionally alert. His coat, pure white, is long and slightly wavy.

Liptok A sheepdog named after the district of Lipto, spelt Leptow in Polish and Luptov in Slovak, in the great Pall of the Tatra Mountains, and closely associated with the Komondor and Kuvasz breeds of Hungary.

At first sight the Liptok's head looks very much like that of the Komondor. The coat is short and smooth on the head, but medium in length on the body. The texture is soft and woolly, and always white.

Old English Sheepdog This attractive dog is sometimes called the Bob-tail Sheepdog, and has a distinctively profuse, shaggy and curl-free coat. In color he may be any shade of gray, grizzle, blue or blue-merle, with or without white markings.

Owtcharka Often called the Russian Sheepdog, he is one of the largest European pastoral dogs, and has often been used as a guard dog as well as for shepherding purposes. In appearance he resembles the Old English Sheepdog, but with longer legs and a shorter back. It is thought that this dog and the Bearded Collie may be part of the ancestry of the Old English Sheepdog.

His coat is shaggy and woolly in texture, often matting and taking on the appearance of the coat of the Komondor. In color he is white, fawn, tawny tawny-and-white or tawny-and-red.

Philippine Islands Dog This is a breed that comes chiefly from the island of Luzon, and also known as the Philippine Edible Dog and the Philippine Native Dog. Although the cooking of this animal will not warrant an entry in a *cordon bleu* cookbook, he was held in high esteem by the tribes of Northern Luzon. The flesh is said to have a better flavour than that of the indigenous wild pig. The dog is well fattened before being killed, then stuffed with rice and herbs and roasted in the embers of a fire!

These dogs are used by some tribes to

Above: the Pyrenean Mountain Dog is a gentle giant, known in America as the Great Pyrenees. He is generally regarded as a French breed, and was used to protect flocks in the Pyrénées from wolves and bears. In France he is known as Chien de Montagne des Pyrénées. He is a faithful, loyal and docile dog, displaying courage and endurance, and is an excellent pet for homes with plenty of space.

Above left: the Puli is a very distinctive dog, with a coat that hangs down in matted tassles all over his body. He has been used for controlling sheep, and has the unusual habit of jumping on their backs in order to get to the other side of the flock. It is a breed that was recognized by the American Kennel Club in 1937.

herd pigs and fowls. They resemble a cross between a Smooth-haired Fox Terrier and a Bull Terrier. The coat is short and smooth on the head, and colors vary from white to dark tan.

Portuguese Cattle Dog There are several types of this dog, depending on the area of that country in which he is used. At one time he was employed in guarding herds from wolves, and for generally driving them from place to place. His coat is harsh and rather short, although smooth about the face. In color he is gray.

Portuguese Sheepdog This is the Sheepdog of the Estrela mountain range in the province of Beira, in the centre of Portugal. He is a heavy dog, making an excellent watchdog and herder, and has even been used to haul small carts.

There are two types of this breed; the Long-haired type (de Pêlo Comprido) and the Short-haired (de Pêlo Curto). There are many colors from white to black, and a mixture of red-and-tan markings.

Puli This is a small, dark dog, excellent as a sheepdog, but tends to be rather nomadic and adventurous. It is a dog that

has become popular in recent years, and recognized by the American Kennel Club since 1937. His coat is woolly, very dense and long, and tends to hang down in matted tassles, particularly around the hindquarters. In color he is reddish-black or almost any shade of gray.

He has the characteristic way of controlling sheep by jumping over their backs. He is not suitable as a family pet, as he is not often fond of strangers or children.

Pumi This is the Hungarian Cattle Dog, and is thought to have arrived in Hungary from Asia about 1,000 years ago. Although similar to the Puli, he differs in certain respects: the Pumi has a shorter and harsher haired coat, with an abundance of trailing hair all over his body. In color he is like the Puli.

Pyrenean Mountain Dog This is a dog of great size and majesty, with a kindly face and disposition. In America, this dog has been known as the Great Pyrenees, and in his native country as Chien de Montagne des Pyrénées, where he was used to protect flocks from wolves and bears.

He is generally regarded as a French

Above: this Pembrokeshire Corgi can trace his origin back to the twelfth century when he was introduced into Britain by Flemish weavers who later migrated to Wales. It is a breed that makes an excellent pet, although they do become snappy, and like to have their own way.

Right: the Shetland Sheepdog, often called the 'Sheltie', is a charming little dog with great endurance. He is ideal as a pet in small homes, and loves children.

breed, but is just as well known on the Spanish side of the Pyrenees, and is also known in the Basque region, south-west of the range. In Pamplona they were used to haul small carts.

The coat of this breed is long and thick, longest on the collar and hindquarters, and shortest on the head and fronts of the legs. The color is usually white, although white with lemon, biscuit, fawn or light tan on the head and ears is known.

Rottweiler A dog named after the town of Rottweil in Southern Germany. This heavy dog is very ancient, and was used by Swabian Knights to hunt boars. He is, in fact, one of the ancient breeds of boar-hunting dogs of Old Germania. His muscular and powerful body is covered with a short and close smooth coat, which is black with distinctive rich mahogany markings on the cheeks, muzzle, chest and legs.

Shetland Sheepdog In appearance, this breed, often called 'Sheltie', is a scaled-down version of the Collie. It is thought that he originated from the Shetland Islands. There, he is ideal as a sheep herder because the sheep in the isles are smaller than those of the mainland.

His records date back to around 1840, and his ancestors are the old Hill Collie from Scotland and the King Charles Spaniel. He is greatly valued by

shepherds for his herding ability. Being a dainty dog he is not so likely to break through snow which has formed a hard surface crust. His kind nature makes him an excellent pet, ideal with children. In color he may be tricolor or black-and-white, blue merle, and sable from gold to mahogany and white.

Welsh Corgi There are two distinct types of this famous Welsh breed who share a common origin: the Pembrokeshire and the Cardiganshire. Corgi means a dwarf dog, although a few Welsh language experts interpret the word as meaning cur.

The Pembroke type is not as ancient a breed as the Cardigan, although he does go back to the twelfth century, when his predecessors were brought to Britain by Flemish weavers, who then went to live in Wales. The breed at that stage looked like a mixture of Pomeranian, Chow Chow, Keeshond and the distinctive Finnish Spitz.

The Cardigan type, however, has Dachshund in him, and appears to have been brought to Wales by the Central European Celts in about 1,200 BC. He can be distinguished from the Pembroke type by his longer tail. He occurs in any color except pure white, while the Pembroke is red, sable, fawn, or black-and-tan, with white markings on the legs, chest and neck.

Chapter 5 Hunting Dogs

The excitement of pursuing wild animals is an instinct in most men, and probably comes from the necessity of early man to chase and kill beasts for food. Nowadays, it is called sport, because the necessity to eat the game for food is not so pressing.

The keenness to hunt, perhaps, was never so great as in the Middle Ages. At that time there were three distinctive types of hunting dog: a massive but relatively fast dog which would pursue and pull down wild game such as bear; a slow scenting hound to trail and rout out wild boar and other game; and a fast dog able to catch and kill the fastest of prey, whether it be deer or rabbit.

Nowadays, there are two classes: long-legged breeds, often called the sight or gaze hounds, using their good vision and exceptional speed to overtake their quarry; and the slower short-legged breeds hunting by smell and following a trail over great distances.

Many of the hunting breeds have long and fascinating histories. Some have ancestors who can be traced back to several thousand years before the birth of Christ, like the distinctive Saluki Hound who was recorded in the tombs of Pharaohs, about 6,000 years ago.

Hounds baying and socializing, horses patiently waiting, hunt masters organizing, and people watching are all part of the atmosphere that preceeds a hunt. Packs of hounds make a spectacular and unforgettable sight, forever giving the impression of movement and activity.

Left: the Akita Inu is not well known, but he is a handsome Japanese dog. At one time the breed was on the verge of extinction but in about 1928 a society was formed in Japan to renew interest in it. In color, examples of this breed may be cream, fawn, red, pale biscuit, black, black-and-tan, and brindle. The breed was imported into Britain during the late Thirties.

Far left: the Afghan Hound is one of the most ancient of all domestic breeds. They are greatly prized for their speed and fearless nature, and at one time were used for hunting in Kabul and Turkestan. This breed was first exhibited in Britain in about 1885, and since then has been popular as a pet. He is able to adapt to most climates, as the weather in his native Afghanistan is very hot in the summer and extremely cold in the winter.

Hunting Breeds

Afghan Hounds There can be few dogs so distinctive and aloof as these majestic creatures. It is an ancient Afghanistan hunting breed, first exhibited in Britain in 1885. With a fine and silky coat, naturally short on the back but long on the flanks, ears and limbs, he is a dog to attract attention wherever he goes.

Records show that he is one the oldest of all domestic breeds, and rock carvings suggest they were in existence at least 4,000 years ago. They were bred in Kabul and Turkestan for hunting, where they are valued for their speed and fearlessness.

So attractive is its coat, with its soft texture, that the wool has been used for gloves and scarves. The very fine hair is hard wearing, especially when mixed with a little sheep wool.

Akita Inu This Japanese hunting dog was introduced into Britain about 1937, and is a member of the Spitz group. It is a very ancient breed and at one time was on the verge of extinction. However, in 1928 a society was formed in Japan to restore interest in them.

They are used for hunting, although the Japanese have used them in time of war as couriers of messages. These attractive

animals are very alert and active and in color can be fawn, cream, pale biscuit, black, red, black-and-tan and brindle. Army dogs are usually dark in color.

Basenji These are members of the hound group, and are unique in the dog world, for instead of barking, they make a distinctive squeal. Their gait, when running, often resembles a racehorse trotting flat out.

Their history goes back many years. At one time they were used by natives in the Southern Sudan and the old Belgian Congo for hunting game. They have keen noses and the ability to run very fast. Like the Afghan Hound their history can be traced back through rock engravings, and they are thought to have been used by the Pharaohs of ancient Egypt.

In play they are lovable and tireless, and excellent with children. Their coats, which are short and silky, are pure bright red, pure black or black-and-tan, with the feet, chest and tail tip colored white.

Bassett Hound The popular and lugubrious Bassett Hound is of French origin, and for his size has a heavier bone structure than any other dog. His lineage goes back many centuries to the old French Bloodhound and the St. Hubert Hound. He has been used both as a badger-hunting.

dog and for hunting truffles, and was first imported into Britain in the 1860s.

The Bassett Hound makes an intelligent, docile, kind and loyal pet, but does need to be controlled by one person only. His long and floppy ears, together with his glum expression, make him an entertaining character to have around the home. The close hound-type coat can be of any hound color, such as black, tan-and-white, or lemon-and-white.

Beagle This is a small hound-type dog, bred for many years in Britain for hare and rabbit hunting. According to legend, Beagles are descended from scent hounds used by King Arthur and his knights. It is known that Queen Elizabeth the First used them for hunting, and that William Shakespeare gave mention to them in some of his works.

In character, Beagles are lively family pets, ideally suited for small homes. Like the Bassett, they have close and hard hound-type coats, in any hound color.

Bloodhound This is a very ancient breed of hound, introduced into Britain about the time of the Norman invasion and used as a tracker dog. He is said to have landed on the English shore with William the Conqueror. However; this Father of all Hounds is able to trace his history back

even further, to Egypt and Greece, centuries before the birth of Christ.

About AD 300, a hound resembling the modern Bloodhound was described by Cladius Aeianus in his *History of Animals*. The hound which he describes was introduced into Europe from Constantinople, now Istanbul, and by the twelfth century had become very popular with hunters.

He was kept by kings and barons, and was introduced into medieval monastery life. This fine hound derives his name Bloodhound from the fact that he was often kept by members of the aristocracy, people who professed to have royal blood in their veins.

The Bloodhound's great ability is to track and follow a scent, at which he is incomparable. Because of his need to be active, he does not make a very good pet for small houses or flats. The color of his coat may be black-and-tan, red-and-tan, or tawny.

Borzoi This beautiful and distinctive hound was bred by the Czars of Russia for pursuing wolves. Indeed, he is also known as the Russian Wolfhound. In about 1705, a member of the Russian nobility imported some Gazelle Hounds or Arabian Greyhounds into Russia for hunting. Unable to withstand the very cold Russian winters, they died. The Duke imported a few more of these dogs, and crossed them with a much tougher native dog, somewhat like the British Collie. The result of this cross is the distinctive and aristocratic-looking dog well able to survive severe weather.

In about 1880, the breed was intro-

duced into Britain, when the late Queen Alexander owned one.

As a pet, Borzoi need plenty of attention and companionship. He shows great affection for his owner and is generally very docile, but he can bite with tremendous speed when provoked. His attractive coat is usually red-and-white or black-and-white.

Coon Hound This is an all-American breed, whose ancestry can be traced back to the Virginian Foxhound, Bloodhound and the American Foxhound. The breed gained recognition with the American Kennel Club in 1945.

Their main quarry is the racoon, but they are also used to hunt the bob-cat and tree bear, which they chase up trees so that the hunters can shoot them.

As hounds they are not very fast, but they are exceedingly tenacious, with the ability to follow a scent for miles.

Dachshund This attractive and popular animal was bred initially for badger hunting in Europe and is said to have been introduced into Britain by Prince Albert. They are intelligent, playful, individualistic, and ideal as family pets.

There are three main types: the Smooth or Short-haired type, which has a short, dense and shiny coat; the Long-haired, with a soft and silky coat; and the Wire-coated, which has a hard coat with a good undercoat.

The Long-haired type is more used to being shown, rather than working as a badger catcher. It is the Wire-haired type which has a long working history, being capable of taking a great deal of punishment when in pursuit of game. Indeed

Left: Fox Hounds love the companionship of their fellow dogs. The pure English Fox Hound is said to have originated in the United States of America in about 1738. Fortunately, records of Fox Hound breeding have been meticulously kept by hunt masters in Britain.

Above: the Bassett Hound is a lovable fellow. Such is his tolerant disposition that it is nearly impossible to annoy him, and therefore he is excellent in homes with children. He takes well to country and town life, but does require plenty of exercise.

Right: these long-haired Dachshunds are delightful pets, bringing excitement and bustle to the whole house. The meaning of Dachshund in German is 'Badger Dog', and indicates the use to which they were originally put.

Far right: the Wire-haired Dachshund has a hard coat, but the undercoat is soft and dense, affording good protection from bad weather. Of all the Dachshunds, the Wire-haired type is the most sporting, having a long history of pursuing game. He has even been used against wild boars and foxes.

Below right: the Short-haired Dachshund has a dense and shiny coat. The Dachshunds are said to have been popularized in Britain by Prince Albert, and are intelligent animals, ideal as family pets.

such is his tenacity, that he was also used against wild boars, wounded deer and foxes.

Deerhound Without a doubt this is a most courageous and ancient breed. Throughout the centuries they have been given many names, such as Scottish Deerhound, The Royal Dog of Scotland, Rough Greyhound, and Highland Greyhound. Looking like a shaggy, wiry-coated greyhound, he can be traced back to the early sixteenth century, when he was a favourite with Scottish Chieftans. About the middle of the eighteenth century, when the Clans broke up, this noble creature became almost extinct.

The speed and strength of Deerhound is legendary, and it has been known for him to bring down a Scottish Deer weighing 113kg (250lbs). He also has the ability to scent game, and is a wonderful tracker. The coat is distinctive, being harsh and wiry, about 7.5-10cm (3-4in) long, and colored dark blue-gray.

Elkhound The history of this attractive animal goes back about 4,000 years to Western Norway. At that time, he was employed to herd flocks and defend them from wolves and bears. He is very intelligent and fearless, with great stamina and energy. His fierce courage makes him a great hunter, especially of elk. Such is his great ability to scent, that he can detect an elk up to 4.8km (3 miles) away.

His coat is dense and hard, lying hard against the body. It can be colored various shades of gray, with black tips to the outer coat. It is lighter in color on the chest, stomach, legs and the underside of the tail.

Finnish Spitz This is one of the most beautiful and attractive of dogs, with a coat of bright reddish-brown or yellowish-red in color. His eagerness to

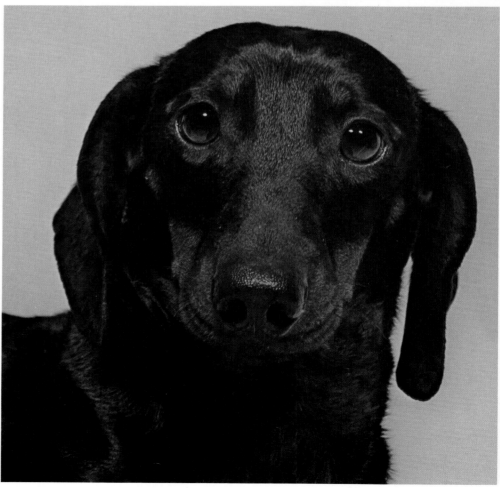

hunt, combined with courage and fidelity, make him an ideal dog. He is also a good family dog and takes great care when cleaning himself. He does not have the 'doggy' smell that so many other dogs have.

Great Dane This noble dog originated in Germany, where he was used for boar hunting. He is thought to be the result of a cross between an English Mastiff and a native German dog of similar appearance. He was then introduced to England to hunt boars, where his tremendous weight, size and endurance made him an ideal pursuer.

He is a dog that needs plenty of room and a great deal of food. His brindle, fawn, blue, black or harlequin colored coat is short, thick and glossy.

Greyhound The oldest known record of this amazing dog is about 4,000 BC, where he is seen as a carving on the tomb of Amten in the valley of the Nile. And even that long ago he was recognizable as the breed we know today. He was

taken to Britain by Mediterranean traders, and is recorded in the Laws of Canute, which were enacted in AD 1,016. Known as the fastest dog in the world, he has been used to hunt many kinds of small game, from hares to foxes, and even deer. But he uses sight only in hunting.

His claim to fame in modern times is on the race track, where he has been trained to chase mechanical rabbits around a set course. When kept as a pet he is very docile and gentle, with a most pleasing character. His coat, which is fine and close, may be black, white, red, blue, fawn, fallow or brindle, or these colors broken with white.

Irish Wolfhound This is probably the most powerful of all dogs, and the great heroic dog of Ireland. His history dates back to about AD 200, when his fame as a fighter was recorded by a Roman Consul. He is a legend in Ireland, and has been written about in battle by poets and playwrights. He is a noble, intelligent and courageous animal, with a dignified appearance.

Above: the Great Dane came from Germany, where he was used for boar hunting. The Saxons introduced this noble beast to Britain to hunt boars.

Above: the Irish Wolfhound is a noble and aristocratic dog, possibly the tallest and most powerful of all members of the canine race. His past is closely linked with Ireland, and he is well recorded by poets and playwrights for his legendary fighting powers. His temperament is gentle and loyal, and he makes an excellent companion and playmate for children.

Right: like the Irish Wolfhound, the Great Dane is good with children, although, because of his size, he may inadvertently knock over a very small child. There is often a wide range of color variations within this breed.

Below: the Saluki's history can be traced back many hundreds of years, and it is thought that they were known 6,000 years ago by the Pharaohs of Egypt. They were so highly treasured at that time that they were laid to rest beside their tombed masters.

Right: the Whippet is a miniature version of a Greyhound. He has been known as the working man's Greyhound, and at one time was used to hunt rabbits in a closed arena. For his weight, the Whippet is the fastest dog in the world, reaching speeds of 56kph (35mph).

Lurcher This is the traditional hunting dog of the poachers, and has been known for several hundred years. The lurcher looks very much like a Greyhound, but in general its coat is harsher and longer, with colors which include brindle, brindle striped with black, black-and-tan, or deep self-slate blue.

Because they were trained as poachers, they had to hunt silently and stealthily, both by sight and scent. It is said that if caught, Lurchers were trained not to give any recognition of their owner.

Plott Hounds This hound owes its name to a German family who in 1750 emigrated to America, taking some of their treasured hounds with them.

It is a dog that shows great courage and stamina at tracking such game as bear and mountain lions. In color they are brindle, with black saddles, and have been registered with the American Kennel Club since 1947.

Rhodesian Ridgeback This is the African Lion Hound or Rhodesian Lion-dog, and his lineage goes back about 300 years to the time of the Huguenots' emigration to South Africa. The dogs they took with them mated with a native, half-wild dog which has a ridge of fur along his back.

He is a friendly, devoted and loyal dog, but tends to work best with just one master. His color is light wheaten to red

wheaten, but a little white on the chest and toes is permissible.

Saluki Often known as the Gazelle Hound, this attractive dog of the Greyhound type may well be the oldest pure-bred dog in existence. Writings found in tombs of the Pharaohs indicate that the Saluki, which originated about 6,000 years ago is very much the animal we know today. So highly was this dog esteemed in those far-off days, that they were often laid to rest alongside their dead masters, so that they could accompany them into the next world.

They were used throughout the Middle East as hunting dogs for game such as gazelle, fox and hare. He is a most noble and dignified dog, with a smooth coat of a soft texture. His coloring can vary, including white, cream, fawn, golden red, grizzle-and-tan, tricolor or black-and-tan, or any variation of these colors.

Whippet This breed is a miniature version of the Greyhound, and probably evolved by crossing the Greyhound with a Manchester Terrier. When bull and bear baiting was banned in Britain, the gentry required a new spectator pasttime, so they developed Whippets to hunt rabbits in closed arenas.

As a pet he is handsome, with a charming disposition, and he delights in being involved with the family.

6 The Terriers

The active and vibrant terriers are often called 'earth dogs', and this is because the word terrier is derived from the Latin word for earth, *terre*.

Terriers are formidable fighters, with great courage and tenacity, and for this reason they were used in conjunction with packs of foxhounds. If the hounds put a fox to earth, terriers were used to drive him out.

These fearless dogs were also used for digging out badgers and for otter-hunting. In hunting the latter, they were employed to find and drive out their prey from holes among the roots of trees along the banks of streams.

The eyes of terriers are quite distinctive, being alert and small. Usually, they are a dark brown in color, sometimes nearly black.

Most vermin live in fear of these dogs, and they are said to kill rats with one snap at the back of the neck. For this reason, they are invaluable on farms, and especially so during harvesting.

The terriers have a long and noble past, being mentioned by Johannes Caius, the physician-in-chief to Queen Elizabeth the First, in his *De Canibus Britannicis* in 1570. Caius mentioned sixteen different types of dog, one of them being the Terrier. The Swedish naturalist Carl von Linné also mentioned the Terrier and its derivation from England in his *Systema Naturea*, published in 1756.

These charming and appealing Fox Terrier puppies will develop into the alert and active adults well known throughout America and Britain. Originally, they were used to drive foxes and other vermin out of confined places, but are now chiefly kept as pets. They are great exhibitionists, full of clowning instinct.

The Terriers

Airedale This is an ancient breed and one of the largest of the terriers. He derives his name from an agricultural show at Bingley, Yorkshire, England, in 1879. Apparently a large group of Waterside Terriers which were exhibited so impressed the judges that they named the breed after the area in which the show was held, Airedale.

He is often called the 'King of the Terriers', being bold and courageous. He is a strong dog, with plenty of power and action. His spirit is high, and his friendliness makes him an ideal family pet. The color of his coat is black or grizzle, with tan, and a texture that is hard, dense, wiry, straight and close.

Australian Terrier This high spirited terrier comes from Australia, and can be traced back to 1885, when he was exhibited in a dog show in Melbourne. The parentage of this, the smallest of all the terriers, is an Australian native dog called the Broken-haired or the Rough-coated Terrier which was crossed with the 'Scottie'. However, other terriers which are thought to be in his lineage are the Cairn, the Dandie Dinmont, the Yorkshire and the Irish. It was in 1896 that he was first introduced into Britain.

In Australia they have been used to herd sheep, and they are superb ratters. Their coats, which are harsh and straight, are colored blue or silver-gray, with tan markings on the head and legs or clear sandy or red.

Bedlington Terrier This is a graceful and lithe muscular dog without any sign of weakness or coarseness. He has a charm-ing and distinctive expression. He is named after the district of Bedlingtonshire in Northumberland, and has been known for 150 years. His ancestors are the Old Border Sleuthhound and the Rough-haired Terrier of the border dales. With a pear or wedged-shaped head, and a back arched at the loin, his appearance is unforgettable.

He is a dog, however, that dislikes other pets receiving attention and praise, and therefore he is best kept as a pet on his own, when he will be loyal and courageous.

Border Terrier This is one of the rarest of the terriers, and comes from the border counties between Scotland and England. He is a fine sporting dog, known in his present form for at least 300 years. As a pet he is delightful, wanting to please his owner at all times. He is also a fine sporting dog, tackling all vermin, including badgers and foxes. His coat is harsh and dense, with a close undercoat, and may be colored red, grizzle, or tan, or blue and tan.

Bull Terrier This is the 'Gladiator of the Dog World', a fearless dog in battle yet delightful with children — even very young ones. He is a dog that was developed in the early 1820s, when the English Bulldog was crossed with the now extinct English Terrier. He was mentioned in the writings of the famous Pierce Egan's *Annals of Sporting* in 1822, when he suggested that it was *a la mode* to have one of these dogs trotting at your heel. At that time, the dog was also known as the 'Half-and-Half'.

He is a dog that was created for fight-ing, ratting and bull baiting. Such was his fame at ratting, that it is said that one dog killed one thousand rats in one hundred minutes.

Their coats, which are short, flat and harsh to the touch but with a fine gloss, are white or white colored, preferably brindle.

Cairn Terrier This is one of the oldest terriers, originating from the Isle of Skye and used since time immemorial in the Highlands against all vermin, including wild cats, otters and foxes. It is thought that King James the First of Scotland owned one in 1605.

As a pet he is a one-man dog, and is a true and loyal friend. His coat is hard and weather resistant, and red, sandy, gray, brindle or nearly black in color.

Dandie Dinmont Terrier This game and hardy terrier is the Old Mustard-and-Pepper dog of the Teviodale region of Britain. The dog we recognise today goes back to 1704, when he appears in a portrait painted by Gainsborough of the third Duke of Buccleuch. This terrier is also given mention in the novels of Sir Walter Scott.

He is hardy and courageous, very friendly and a fine family dog, although he does need to be trained early in his life. His coat is crisp, and in color from a pepper dark blue-black to silver-gray, to mustard, and from reddish brown to pale fawn.

Fox Terrier This is a very fashionable terrier, known widely throughout America and Britain. There are two distinct types, the Smooth-coated and the Wire-coated. The Smooth-coated Fox

Above: this Wire-haired Fox Terrier is an alert animal, keen to be involved in the pursuit of vermin. The Wire-haired type is a much older breed than the Smooth-haired one, and his origin can be traced back to the mid-eighteenth century. His distinctive coat is dense and wiry with crisp whiskers.

Terrier was first recorded in about 1790, but it was not until the middle of the nineteenth century that he appeared in the form we know today. Included in his ancestors are the Beagle, Smooth-coated Black-and-tan Terriers, and the Greyhound.

The Wire-haired Fox Terrier is older than the Smooth type, and is known to have been used to root out foxes from their lairs.

The Smooth-haired Fox Terrier has a straight, flat and smooth coat, while the Wire-haired type has a coat that is dense and wiry, but not curled.

Glen of Immal Terrier This ancient Irish terrier is extremely rare, and gains his name from the Immal Glen in County Wicklow. At one time he was used in dog fights, upon which bets were placed. However, he is now no more than a house dog.

He was first exhibited at an Irish Kennel Club Show in Dublin in 1933. In stature he is quite small, with short legs in compari-

son with the rest of his body. In color he may be wheaten, blue, brindle or blue and tan.

Irish Terrier This remarkable terrier from the Emerald Isle is well tempered with humans, lithe and active. He makes a good family pet. His coat is dense and wiry, and in color solid bright-red, red-wheaten, or golden-wheatened with no white except a patch on the chest.

Kerry Blue Terrier Another terrier from Ireland is this excellent all-round dog: he makes a superb hunter of small game and a good farm dog. In temperament he can often be stubborn, and his fickle temper makes him prone to bite. Nevertheless, he is a dog of great character.

His coat is deep slate to light blue-gray, with a dense, soft and wavy appearance.

Lakeland Terrier This tireless and sure-footed hunting dog of the English Fells is one of the oldest working terriers. He is descended from the same stock as the Bedlington and the Dandie Dinmont Ter-

riers. They make delightful and adorable pets for the home, and this, combined with a deep bark, makes them useful as guard dogs.

They come in a number of different colors, such as black-and-tan, blue-and-tan, self red, self wheaten and red grizzle. The coat, which is weather resistant, is harsh, wiry and dense.

Manchester Terrier This distinctive animal was famous as a ratting dog in the days when rat-killing contests were held. His ancestors are said to be the Black-and-tan Terrier and a Whippet bitch. He is a dog with a quick manner, making an intelligent house pet. His coat is smooth, dense and glossy, and a jet-black and rich tan in color.

Norwich Terrier This is one of the smallest of the terriers, and a demon for his size. There are two distinct types of this breed: one has drop-ears and is called the Norfolk Terrier; the other with prick-ears is the Norwich Terrier. Also, the coat of the Norfolk's is usually shorter than that of the Norwich's. The coats are red and red-wheaten, black-and-tan, or grizzle.

It was back in the 1860s that Colonel Vaughan hunted a pack of small red terriers bred from the Irish Terrier in Ballybrick, as it was then called, Southern Ireland. The early breeders of these dogs were not concerned with the different types of ear posture they were producing, as at that time they were only interested in the dogs for working purposes. It was not until they were exhibited at shows that the ear difference became apparent.

Scottish Terrier This world-famous dog can be traced back to the Isle of Skye and the West Coast of Scotland. He is a strong and alert little dog, highly strung and with extremely powerful teeth. Although a one-man dog, he will associate with children if brought up with them. His coat is a handsome black, wheaten or brindle, and intensely hard and wiry.

Sealyham Terrier This dog comes from the coast of Permbrokeshire, West Wales. He is named after the estate of his breeder, Sealyham, in the borough of Haverfordswest. His ancestors are the Welsh Pembrokeshire Corgi, Dandie

Above: at one time the Tibetan Terrier was used by Tibetans to round up stray sheep from steep mountain slopes. They are attractive little dogs with an alert and affectionate disposition.

Right: the West Highland Terrier is a fellow full of confidence and self importance, and makes an ideal one-man dog. He originated in Argyllshire in Scotland during the early nineteenth century, and has been popular ever since. His coat tends to shed badly over carpets and furniture, which can be a nuisance in many homes.

Dinmont, West Highland White Terrier, and the Bull Terrier, and it is recorded that in 1850 he was used in the hunting of otters, foxes and badgers.

Skye Terrier This delightful dog comes from the Isle of Skye. He is an obedient and loyal dog, but tends to be a one-man animal. Often they become neurotic, and require lots of love and affection. In color they are dark or light blue gray, fawn or cream.

Soft-coated Wheaten Terrier This clear, wheaten-colored terrier has been known in Ireland for sometime, and is officially recognized by the Irish Kennel Club. He is an extremely game and plucky terrier, hardy, but sweet and gentle as well. His coat is soft and dense, and curled or wiry.

Staffordshire Bull Terrier This fiercesome dog was bred to bait bulls in pits, and is thought to have derived from the crossing of Bulldogs and the Old English Black-and-tan hard-haired Terrier.

He is a dog that is often docile and good tempered, but when aroused he is like a tiger, and will fight to the death. His coat is short, stiff and glossy. In color it may be a variety of hues, such as red, fawn, white, black or blue. It may also be white, or brindle with white.

Sydney Silky Terrier A small, game and intelligent Australian terrier that originated near Sydney, New South Wales. He is believed to be descended from crossing an Australian Terrier and a Yorkshire Terrier, from which the silky coat was derived. In color his coat may be slate blue, blue-and-tan, or sandy red.

Tibetan Terrier This charming little terrier comes from Tibet, and along with the Shih Tzu and Lhaso Apso has an ancient history. The Tibetan Terrier makes an excellent pet, with a soft and waved coat that can be cream, gray, black or part-colored.

Welsh Terrier As a pure bred dog this terrier's ancestry goes back to 1850, when he was used to hunt otters, badgers and foxes. Nowadays, however, he is kept as a pet. His high spirits are often liked by children, with whom he is affectionate.

West Highland White Terrier This terrier originated from the estate of the Malcolms of Poltalloch in Argyllshire, Scotland, during the first part of the nineteenth century. He is an individualistic terrier, exhibiting an air of great self-importance. He is quite definitely a one-man dog. His white coat is quite hard and free from curl.

Toy and Small Dogs

Toy and other small dogs are some of the most delightful and adaptable dogs, and are especially suited as pets for apartments and small houses. They have been selected and bred often solely for pleasure and amusement, and therefore some of the breeds are highly strung and neurotic. But all are lovable, delightful and amusing pets.

Many of these toy and small dogs have distinguished pasts, and several of them are from the Orient.

A number of small dogs are officially classified by the British Kennel Club as Toys. There are, of course, many other breeds that are just as distinctive and individualistic, making superb pets for the home. Rather than considering how other people have classified a dog, it is often better to use your own judgement regarding the suitability of a particular breed for your home and family. But remember that as they are small they may need several meals a day instead of one. However, they must not be overfed as many of them will suffer ill health if fat and lethargic.

Although they are small, these delightful dogs often make good guard dogs, and for their size may display far more fortitude than many larger members of the canine race.

The Chihuahua is the tiniest dog in the world. It is believed that the ancestors of this diminutive breed ran wild in packs of fifty or more in Mexico, living on young birds and rodents. Nowadays, they are more at home on a soft cushion or on a lap. Nevertheless, they are active and lively, making amusing and endearing pets.

Above: the attractive and individualistic King Charles Spaniel is an excellent family pet. There are four color variations within this breed: black-and-tan (King Charles), white-black-and-tan (Prince Charles), red-and-white (Blenheim), and red (Ruby). The variation pictured here is the Prince Charles type.

Left: the Maltese dog comes, as his name suggests, from the island of Malta in the Mediterranean Sea. His coat is long and straight, silky and pure white. He is very affectionate and loves attention and companionship.

Some Toy Dogs

Black-and-Tan Terrier This delightful little dog is often known as the English Toy Terrier, and in many ways looks like a small version of the Manchester Terrier. He is an alert and energetic fellow, barking at every sound.

He has the virtues of having a coat which does not shed, and he is free of any 'doggy' odour. His smooth and glossy black-and-tan coat is attractive, and he is an excellent pet, especially for small houses, becoming a lively character.

Cavalier King Charles Spaniel Of all the small dogs, these are perhaps some of the most adorable and lovable. They are gay and lively in disposition, almost to the point of being bumptious. They adore children, and are as equally at home running around a garden or park as being curled up in a chair in front of a fire.

It is a very old breed and closely associated with the King Charles Spaniel. When it became fashionable to breed King Charles Spaniels with short noses, the old type with long noses, fine-pointed muzzles and flat-topped skulls started to disappear, and only occasionally were any seen. In the 1920s a group of breeders decided to revive and reintroduce the old and original type, and this slowly began to build up stock of the early type. In 1928, the breed Cavalier King Charles Spaniel was registered — the word Cavalier indicating that it is distinguished from the flat-nosed King Charles Spaniels.

In color they may be black-and-tan, ruby (a rich red), Blenheim (chestnut-and-white), and tricolor. The coat is long and silky, but free from curl. However, a slight wave is permissible.

Chihuahua A Mexican dog and probably the smallest breed in the world. These diminutive dogs are often tender, though at the same time they are refined and delicate. The coat is short and smooth, and seldom shed.

Because of this small size, he is not suitable as company for children, as there

Right: the Pug is a small dog displaying courage and fortitude. He has no 'doggy' odour and does not need a great deal of grooming. The Pug was first introduced into Britain in 1884, and since then has been popular. It is a breed that is not good with small children, but quite tolerant of those older than, say, six, who are able to give him the attention he craves.

Far right: the Pekingese is known the world over, and has a lineage that goes back about 2,000 years. They were so highly prized at one time that they were cared for by slave-girls and eunuchs. They spread from China after the English looted the Imperial Palace in Peking in 1860. Pekingese are individualistic dogs needing plenty of attention.

is the chance that he may be trodden upon or squashed. The coat is usually white, but it can be any other color or a mixture of colors.

Griffon Bruxellois A Belgian toy dog that has become very popular throughout the Continent. The ancestors of this breed go back many years; it appears in a fifteenth century painting by Jan van Eyck called *Giovanni Arnolfini and His Bride*. His parentage is uncertain, but it is thought that he comes from a cross between the Belgian Sheepdog and the German Affenpinscher. However, the Ruby Spaniel and the Pug are also in his ancestry.

Italian Greyhound This miniature Greyhound, as his name indicates, comes from Italy, where he is called the Piccolo Levriere Italiano. It is known from paintings that he has remained in his present form for the past 2,000 years, and was liked by Egyptian, Greek and Roman nobility. Throughout his years he has been a great favourite with painters. This breed travelled to England in the early seventeenth century and was very popu-

lar during the Victorian period.

They are gentle and affectionate animals, but they do need warmth. In color they may be red, blue, fawn, cream, white, black-and-fawn, or white pied. The coat is thin and glossy.

Japanese These dogs originated in China, not Japan, and travelled to Britain when Commodore Perry gave a couple to Queen Victoria. These attractive animals can be traced back 2,000 years, and at one time they were raised by Japanese royalty and given to foreigners who had rendered outstanding service to that country.

Often known as Japanese Spaniels, they are delightful dogs, with long, straight and silky coats but no wave or curl. In color they may be red-and-white or black-and-white.

King Charles Spaniel This is an old breed, and one from which the Cavalier King Charles Spaniel is descended. Many people believe that this attractive dog originated during the reign of King Charles II, but he is much older than that. He can be traced back to the Japan of

Above: the Jack Russell Terrier was developed by Parson Jack Russell from Devon, England. The first Jack Russell Terriers differed from the breed we know today, being much larger. The present-day terriers are impish and mischievous, digging holes and investigating all corners. Indeed, they were bred for digging out vermin and going down burrows.

Right: the Papillon is admirably described — the French word meaning butterfly. Their fringed ears, together with a blaze on the head, make them look very much like delicate butterflies. They are lively dogs, full of happiness and fun.

2,000 BC. It is not clear how he came to Britain, but it is known he was a great favourite with King Charles II. But prior to that he was also a favourite with King Henry VIII and was mentioned by the physician to Queen Elizabeth the First. King Charles I also had these dogs, but it was his son who made them famous.

Unfortunately, after the fall of the Stuarts they were banned at the English Court, but many were still kept in country houses. During Victorian times they enjoyed a revival, and Queen Victoria kept one called 'Dash'.

They are compact and refined animals, with four color variations to their coats: black-and-tan (King Charles), white-black-and-tan (Prince Charles), red-and-white (Blenheim), and red (Ruby).

Maltese As the name suggests, this dog is named after the island of Malta, and has been a favourite and aristocratic fellow for nearly 3,000 years. He is one of the most attractive of the small dogs, with a pure white long, straight and silky coat.

Papillon The French name papillon admirably describes his personality and appearance. They are gay and vivacious animals with large fringed ears that together with the white blaze on the head gives the appearance of a butterfly.

They are not robust dogs, and must be exercised and fed carefully. Their coats may be either two-colored or tricolored, and are usually white-and-black, white-and-sable, or white and a shade of red, or white-and-black with tan spots.

Pekingese This is a breed that goes back about 2,000 years. Around that time in China they were known as the Lion-dogs of Peking, and were specially cared for by slave-girls and eunuchs. In 1860 the Imperial Palace in Peking was looted by the English and some of these delightful and distinctive dogs were taken away and subsequently introduced into Europe and Britain.

The Pekingese are individualists and seldom make friends easily. They are certainly not dogs for a family home with children.

They may be any color, such as red, fawn, black, black-and-tan, white, cream, sable, or brindle, and any color can have a black mask on the face. The coat is often coarse, but straight and flat and never curly or wavy.

Pomeranian The Pomeranian owes his ancestry to the Spitz-type sled dogs of Iceland and Lapland. However, he derives his name from Pomerania, a former province of north-east Germany, which is now in north-west Poland. The breed was popularized in 1875 when Queen Victoria owned one.

They are excellent pets for small houses, being active and very obedient. However, it is a breed that needs early and thorough training if they are not to exert their own will in the house.

Pug These distinctive dogs originated in the Far East and were introduced into Britain in 1884. Dutch traders from the Dutch East India Company are said to be

responsible for their introduction into Europe, and they were soon to become fashionable with the nobility.

He is a square and cobby dog, with a large head and a short, blunt muzzle. Their coats are smooth, short and glossy, and in color they can be silver, apricot, fawn or black.

Yorkshire Terrier This one-man dog's origin is not clear, but he appears to be descended from the Black-and-tan Terrier and the Skye Terrier. It is also believed that the Dandie Dinmont and the Maltese are in his ancestry.

He is a delightful pet for the home, being lovable as well as fearless. His coat is dark steel-blue, black-and-tan, and straight with a silky texture.

Miniature Dogs

There are, in addition to dogs formally classified as Toy Dogs, those which are small and as equally delightful, and perhaps even more interesting. Like the Toys, many can also make good house dogs for small homes and apartments.

Affenpinscher This haughty and proud dog has the German nickname 'monkey terrier' because of his coat which is shaggy and dense in parts.

His ancestry can be traced back to the beginning of this century and he is related to the Griffon Bruxellois and the Miniature Pinscher.

If you ever need a good, small guard dog, then consider this fearless dog, which has the courage of a lion. He also has a sharp bark, an asset for any guard dog.

Australian Silky Terrier This is one of Australia's best-loved dogs — a cross between an Australian Terrier and a Yorkshire Terrier. Brimming with fun and excitement, he is tireless and yappy, but a good friend and an excellent house dog. In color he is blue-and-tan or gray-blue-and-tan, with a silky, flat glossy coat.

Chinese Crested Dog This is a dog that has recently become more popular and although looking slightly bizarre he is very likable.

On his head there is a crest, with more hair on the feet and at the end of the tail. Except for these areas, the dog is entirely hairless. For this reason, he has to be protected from extremes of temperature, and to be kept out of strong sunlight,

Left: Poodles are very chic dogs, radiating a superior attitude to most other dogs. They are superb actors, and like nothing better than to perform before an audience. However, they are often highly strung and neurotic.

Above: the Miniature Pinscher is a small and elegant little dog. He is stylish, full of life and eager to impress his owner or visitors. Because of this he is often difficult to train, and can be cocky and aggressive.

Above: the Shih Tzu is a very ancient Tibetan breed, with a lively disposition and distinctive arrogant carriage. It is a breed with an abundance of hair, with short, muscular legs.

Far right: the Miniature Schnauzer is a smaller version of his larger brother. The standard dog is between 48-50cm (18-19in) high, while the miniature version is 32-35cm (12-13in). Both of these Schnauzers are highly intelligent, and have been referred to as the dogs with a human brain.

especially during summer months.

Jack Russell Terrier This bouncy and vivacious terrier owes his name to Parson Jack Russell, who bought and bred a pack of sporting terriers. Jack Russell was very keen that his terriers should be 'dead game', and this he certainly achieved.

Jack Russell Terriers are fearless little dogs, and in fights will often compete with dogs three times their size. As yet, they have not been recognized by the British Kennel Club, but this in no way diminishes their virtue as good and friendly house dogs, as well as being good ratters and mice catchers.

Miniature Bull Terrier This miniature gladiator of the dog world closely resembles his big brother. In height he is not more than 36cm (14in) high at the shoulder, and has a weight of under 9kg (20lb).

Miniature Long-haired Dachshund This is a gay, bold and highly intelligent dog, which, despite its size, is usually active. He should be like his larger counterpart, but only 3-4kg (7-9lb) in weight.

The coat should be only slightly waved, but for preference straight, and at its longest under the neck and the body and behind the ears.

Miniature Smooth-haired Dachshund Like the long-haired dachshund, this is just a miniature version of the Smooth-haired Dachshund. In weight they should not exceed 5kg (11lb).

Miniature Pinscher This is a sturdy, compact and elegant dog with a smooth coat. In color he is black, blue, chocolate or red, with tan markings on the face.

Miniature Poodle These are very popular and chic dogs, often being associated with ladies, when they serve admirably as lap dogs. In appearance they are exact counterparts of their larger relatives: the miniatures are 38cm (15in) at the shoulder and the toys 23cm (11in) or under.

These dogs are great actors and enjoy having an audience. In fact they are often very highly strung and neurotic. They will need clipping, and this is best left to an expert, especially when the animals are very young.

Miniature Schnauzer Like his larger relative, the miniature Schnauzer is robust with a square appearance. He is about 33cm (13in) high at the shoulder.

He is full of character, bold and very reliable, with a cobby appearance and a deep chest.

Shih Tzu This lively and alert dog has a distinctively arrogant carriage. In weight he is 26-35kg (12-16lb) and in size 23cm (10in) at the shoulder.

They have a profuse coat evenly distributed over their bodies, with especially long and abundant whiskers and beard.

Index

Page numbers in italics refer to illustrations

Acknowledgements
The publishers would like to thank the following photographic agencies for their kind permission to reproduce photographs in this book:
Bruce Coleman Limited: 6/7, 8/9, 11, 12, 12/13, 18, 21, 22, 22/23, 24, 26, 27 (top and bottom right), 28, 29, 33, 34, 37 (top left), 38, 39 (top), 47, 50 (top right), 52/53, 54, 58, 58/59, 60, 63, 68/69, 70 (top and bottom), 71, 74, 76/77, 80, 83, 87, 88, 89, 90 (top and bottom right), 91, 92/93, 93 and 94.
Zefa Picture Library (U.K.) Limited: Front and end papers, 2/3, 4/5, 10, 14 (top and bottom), 15, 16, 17, 19, 20, 25, 30/31, 32, 35, 36, 37 (bottom left), 39, 40, 41, 42/43, 44, 45, 46, 48, 48/49, 50 (bottom right), 51, 55, 56, 57, 61, 62, 64/65, 66, 67, 69, 72, 73 (top and bottom), 74/75, 78, 79, 81, 82, 84/85, 86 and 95.

Front cover: Bruce Coleman Limited
Back cover: Bruce Coleman Limited